YOU YOUR MONEY & GOD

"Biblical Standards for relating to Money"

TONY ALEOGENA-RAPHAEL

Copyright © 2019

YOU, YOUR MONEY
A N D G O D
TONY ALEOGENA-RAPHAEL

ISBN: **9789789811748**

Published by: Chorus Media

CONTENTS

DEDICATION

To my wife and daughter – Temi & Angel.

THANK YOU

Writing a book is harder than I thought and more rewarding than I could have imagined. Several people made contributions that made my job a little easier and I would like to use this opportunity to appreciate a few of them.

This period in my life was filled with many ups and downs and I needed a bit of motivation to keep going at times. My family, especially wife and daughter were always on hand to urge me on when I needed a little lift, excusing extended time alone in my study and showering me with genuine affection. Thank you.

A very special thanks to my pastor and mentor for making time out of his busy schedule – in the middle of two book projects of his own, to read through the manuscript, offering advice and write the forward of this book. I can't thank you enough sir.

To Idara Edwin for the initial edit work and for offering important suggestions and helping to give form to some of the early ideas.

And to my irrepressible editor Iniobong Afahakan thank you for your editorial work, keen insights and many ideas and suggestions.

To Awaji Tontex and Inem Inyang-Ito for the cover and page designs.

To my staff and associates, thank you. I appreciate your show of support at every point.

And to everyone at City Church Calabar, you gave me the courage to write this book. You Rock!

FOREWORD

Money is a hot-button subject everywhere and at all times. There are many books already on the subject of money: how to make, manage and multiply it. I should alert you though that You, Your Money & God is not just another book, it adds another dimension to our understanding of the subject. It addresses the basics and then takes us further. I like the fact that the author boldly confronts current issues emanating from the intersection of the Church and money including tithing, accountability, remuneration for ministers of the gospel, and the role of the Church in national economy.

Money as a means of exchange for value either for products or services remains one of the remarkable human inventions and it plays a crucial role in our daily living. Money is important and the use makes it easier to have our needs met and to accomplish our goals. One of the things you will find in this book is the assertion that some of the means for acquiring money that we have been taught over the last few decades won't work. Making money depends rather on your acumen.

There are divergent opinions as to whether money is intrinsically evil or a blessing from God; and whether a man ought to desire riches or to be contented with little. The truth is God is rich, and he doesn't have a problem with money, neither does he have a problem with man having wealth. God has given us capacity to create wealth, but not only for our enjoyment and certainly not for flaunting. He blesses us to bless others and to influence culture. Heaven records what we do for man as being done for God. We lay up treasures in eternity when we use money God's way.

As good as it is to acquire wealth, it is important to beware of pride, greed and self-centredness as these have a high potential risk to drift our attention away from God and what He will have us do. Proverbs 11:23 says, "Those who trust in their riches will fall, but the righteous will thrive like a green leaf." When we gain a better understanding of God's perspective on the concept of money and the purpose for which He wants us blessed, we can overcome our ostentatious desires and gain control over money with the help of the Holy Spirit. We cannot serve God and Mammon.

I have watched the author, Tony Aleogena-Raphael, in the process of learning and testing the principles in this book for close to three decades. He has a treasure trove of experiences on what works and what doesn't. There is no doubt that this book will help sharpen your perspective about money and your relationship with God, and more importantly, align you more with God's purpose for your life. Please read with an open mind.

Sam Adeyemi
Daystar Christian Centre, Lagos, Nigeria.

Introduction

"A wise person should have money
in their head, but not in their heart."

Jonathan Swift (1667 – 1775)
Anglo-Irish Poet and Cleric.

Introduction

oney is a hot topic any day, in any culture. No one can understate the importance and the power of its influence over people. Nations have gone to war; many marriages and families have been torn apart by money and possessions than by any other issue.

The subject of money gets even trickier when we introduce God into the equation. Religion and money may be the most explosive combo you can ever have; yet one cannot go without the other. There is nothing intrinsically evil about money. Some people misquote the Bible by saying that money is the root of all evils. But the Bible says it is the love of money that is the root of all kinds of evil. In the right hands, money can do a great deal of good; and in the wrong hands, it can do a lot of evil. The way we use it and our attitude towards it is what makes the difference.

Over the years criticisms have been growing about the seeming commercialization of the gospel to the point that people are now complaining openly even within the pews about the excesses of some church leaders and their rock-star status as well as the skewed theology on money. Therefore many ordinary Christians have become confused about what they ought to believe and do.

This rapid erosion of the credibility of the church and the mockery of the gospel leaves me incensed frequently and I feel deeply impressed in my heart that God wants me to do something about it. The challenge to play a role led me to a period of prayer and research. My mission with this book is to first, clarify some of the contentious issues about money and second is to shape the attitude of Christians towards it.

If you are a Christian, do you know that God has a plan for your money? Maybe no one has ever told you that; but it is true. Following God's plan will bring you financial peace. God promises that following His plan will lead to blessings. However, the blessing is not to make you financially wealthy – but to make you a new person. God's plan for your money is not to make you rich; it is to empower you to do great things in the world for His glory. God's desire for you is that your life will be meaningful. He wants your life to count – to make the greatest possible impact wherever you go.

God also knows and recognizes the power of money to control lives. He knows that money is on our mind a lot; so much that Jesus spoke and taught about it more than any other topic!

But what exactly is God's plan? Why is the concept of tithing so contentious, and how should we relate to money? What if being rich has little to do with how much money we have or don't have? What if the things we associate with having more money or think a lot of money will give us, are just a pipe dream or chasing the wind? How might the Nigerian church restore probity, accountability and respect among her ranks? This book will provide a proper frame for the relationship between God on the one hand, and you and your money on the other hand.

The blessing is not to make you financially wealthy – but to make you a new person. God's plan for your money is not to make you rich; it is to empower you to do great things in the world for His glory.

I have no doubt in my mind that we are in the early days of some seismic activity that will erupt in a national rebirth beginning with the correction of the church. My prayer is that every church leader, pastor, bishop and members will read this book and be courageous enough to re-align themselves with the mind of God wherever there is a need to do so. I pray that the Lord God of Heaven will use this humble work to help touch and transform His church and our nation

Chapter One

"Don't hoard treasure down here where it gets eaten by moths and corroded by rust or – worse! – stolen by burglars. Stockpile treasure in heaven, where it's safe from moth and rust and burglars. It's obvious, isn't it? The place where your treasure is, is the place you will most want to be, and end up being."

Jesus Christ

How God Sees Money

Money plays a significant role in our lives. It's hard not to think about it no matter how much of it we have or don't have. We always worry about not having enough of it or thinking of how to gain more or how to better manage what we already have.

King Solomon, the third king of ancient Israel, once said: *"Money answers all things."*[1] While that may be a hyperbole (meaning it should not be taken literally), it highlights the exalted status of money and its impact on the life of everyone.

For a Christian, this may pose a challenge – balancing the need for financial success and being spiritual. Many people think these two are incompatible. While some believe that being financially successful is an act of God's favour and an essential benefit of the New Covenant in Christ, others consider its relentless pursuit as an unnecessary distraction that can quickly derail a faithful adherent of the faith.

From Jesus' statement quoted at the beginning of this chapter, He doesn't condemn having money. Having a lot of money (or the lack of it) is not a matter of spirituality. It is not a matter of one's religious beliefs but rather, one's acumen. A cursory look at the teachings of Jesus (especially His parables) shows that He spoke more about money than any other subject. He taught more about money than He did about heaven or hell. However, His emphasis was not on how to make more money or how to manage what you have, but on how to relate to money.

Having a lot of money (or the lack of it) is not a matter of spirituality. It is not a matter of one's religious beliefs but rather, one's acumen.

Whether we have a lot of money or not, isn't the question; its place in our lives is what matters to God. One thing is sure, though – you have a worldview and so do I. The way we see the world determines the way we live our lives. How you view

Whether we have a lot of money or not, isn't the question; its place in our lives is what matters to God.

money will determine how you relate to it. So, the question then should be: how should we view money, and what should determine the place of money in our lives?

The answer to that question is simple. We should see money the way God sees it. When we see as God sees, we will be more inclined to do as God says.

How then does God see money? Jesus reveals this in a parable He told His disciples which was directed at the rich and wealthy religious rulers of His days. Leading up to this parable, these religious leaders had berated Jesus who was frequently at odds with them for the company He was keeping. To the Pharisees, it was strange that any rabbi worth his salt would even want to associate with tax collectors and sinners – much less visit their home and dine with them.

Jesus overheard their murmurs and in a bid to help them understand God's mind towards a sinner, He told a trilogy. The three short stories were to help illustrate His point - the story of the lost sheep, the story of a lost coin and finally, the story of a lost son.

After these stories, these men made to leave but Jesus still had a lot to say. He decided to touch on a hot topic – money. He was sure this would interest them because most of them were rich. So just as they made to leave, Jesus said to His disciples (but well within their earshot),

"There was a certain rich man who had a steward, and an accusation was brought to him that this man was wasting his goods..."[2]

As expected, He got their attention.

This factious story, often referred to as the parable of the Shrewd Steward or the Unjust Manager, is a puzzling and confusing story for many; largely because Jesus chose to make a crook the star of the story (which I think was for a shock-effect). Jesus uses this story to communicate at least five fundamental kingdom principles about money. The rich man in the story represents God, while the steward represents man. Read with me:

"He also said to His disciples: "There was a certain rich man who had a steward, and an accusation was brought to him that this man was wasting his goods. So he called him and said to him, 'what is this I hear about you? Give an account of your stewardship, for you can no longer be steward.' Then the steward said within himself, 'what shall I do? For my master is taking the stewardship away from me. I cannot dig; I am ashamed to beg. I have resolved what to do, that when I am put out of the stewardship, they may receive me into their houses.' So he called every one of his master's debtors to him, and said to the first, 'How much do you owe my master?' And he said, 'A hundred measures of oil.' So he said to him, 'Take your bill, and sit down quickly and write fifty.' Then he said to

another, 'And how much do you owe?' So he said, 'A hundred measures of wheat.' And he said to him, 'Take your bill, and write eighty.' So the master commended the unjust steward because he had dealt shrewdly. For the sons of this world are shrewder in their generation than the sons of light. And I say to you, make friends for yourselves by unrighteous mammon, that when you fail, they may receive you into an everlasting home. He who is faithful in what is least is faithful also in much; and he who is unjust in what is least is unjust also in much. Therefore, if you have not been faithful in the unrighteous mammon, who will commit to your trust the true riches? And if you have not been faithful in what is another man's, who will give you what is your own? No servant can serve two masters; for either he will hate the one and love the other, or else he will be loyal to the one and despise the other. You cannot serve God and mammon."3

Principle 1: Ownership is a Myth

"There was a certain rich man who had a steward, and an accusation was brought to him that this man was wasting his goods..."2

Right off the bat in the very first verse is the first principle. Ownership is an illusion. Your possession is not yours after all; it's a trust. God is the real owner and we're just managers. This is a regular theme

Everything we have has been entrusted to us by God.

owner and we're just managers. This is a regular theme

in Jesus' teachings about possession. Everything we have has been entrusted to us by God.

Did I just hear you say, *"But I earned it with my own sweat!* Really?! Who gave you the breath, the health, abilities, aptitude, strength and opportunities that you employed to get what you got? God!

You see, God doesn't give up ownership of a thing even when He gives it to us. All the things we have are merely gifts from God who still retains ownership while allowing us to enjoy them at His pleasure.

God knows the temptation for man is to take credit for his success. The words He spoke to ancient Israelites are still relevant and instructive today. He warned them about developing a strong-headed, self-reliant and disobedient attitude about wealth and its acquisition:

"Beware that you do not forget the Lord your God…. lest – when your heart is lifted….then you say in your heart, 'My power and the might of my hand have gained me this wealth'…remember the Lord your God, for it is He who gives you power to get wealth…."[4]

David, the most successful king of Israel, understood this a long time ago when he prayed to God after the entire nation of Israel brought offerings for the building of the temple in Jerusalem:

"Both riches and honour come from You, and You reign over all. In your hand is power and might; In Your hand, it

is to make great and to give strength to all. … But who am I, and who are my people, that we should be able to offer so willingly as this? For all things come from you and of Your own we have given to you…"[5]

It's so easy to confuse ownership with stewardship. For instance, if you were given a $100 bill and asked to give it to someone else, you would probably do so without a second thought. However, if you were asked to reach into your pocket, pull out the same amount and give it to someone else, you probably wouldn't be that willing. The question now is: Why would you freely give on one circumstance and hesitate on the other? The answer is this: Because of the principle of "ownership vs stewardship."

In the first instance, you were in possession of something that wasn't yours; hence, you did not hesitate to give it away when asked to. In the second instance, seeing yourself as the owner of the $100 bill conferred on you the 'right' to either transfer or withhold possession. The owner has 'rights' while the steward has 'responsibilities'.

Our ability to discern the difference between ownership and stewardship is what determines our being 'rich' or 'poor' in spirit.

Our ability to discern the difference between ownership and stewardship is what determines our being 'rich' or 'poor' in spirit.

If you see yourself as an owner, the first thing you will claim are your rights to do whatever you wish with your possessions and this is what leads to being entitled (i.e. having a sense of entitlement). But if you see yourself as a steward, then the first thing you claim is the fact that what you possess isn't yours and that you will do whatever the owner wants you to do with it. This, on the other hand, is what leads to being 'poor in spirit' (which Jesus spoke about in the gospel). This was David's disposition in the scripture we read earlier. He simply saw himself as a steward with no rights over the things he possessed.

Principle 2: Money is a Trust

The next principle is in the second verse of our reference text:

> It's only normal that stewardship comes with accountability.

"So he called him and said to him, 'what is this I hear about you? Give an account of your stewardship, for you can no longer be steward.'"[6]

God has a plan and a purpose for the money He gave you in trust; therefore, you will have to render an account someday. God will call you to give account and balance the books. This is an obvious principle, isn't it? It's only normal that stewardship comes with accountability.

As a manager, you will at some point be expected to

render account to your principal. We need to constantly remind ourselves of this: that we are supposed to take and follow the instructions of the owner in applying what he has entrusted to us. That there's going to be an audit on our lives - how we used not just our money, but everything that God gave to us. What did you do with what you were given – your talents, your relationships, your opportunities, your mind, your creativity, your contacts, your networks, etc.?

Apostle Paul wrote to the Church in Corinth,

"…it is required in stewards that one be found faithful."[7]

Note that the audit principle is not just limited to our referenced story. In a similar story in Matthew 25:14-30, Jesus repeats that there will be a day when the owner will look into the books and reward everyone accordingly. Living with this mentality will definitely shape our approach towards the allocation of resources under our care.

At the end of your life on earth, you will be evaluated and rewarded according to how well you handled what God entrusted to you. If you treat everything as a trust, God promises three rewards in eternity:

- Affirmation. He will say, *"Good job! Well done!"*
- Promotion and a greater responsibility in eternity. *"…I will put you in charge of…"*

○ Honour and celebration. *"…Come and share your Master's happiness."*[8]

Principle 3: Money as a Tool

The third principle is found in the eighth and ninth verses of our reference text:

"So, the master commended the unjust steward because he had dealt shrewdly. For the sons of this world are shrewder in their generation than the sons of light. "And I say to you, make friends for yourselves by unrighteous mammon, that when you fail, they may receive you into an everlasting home."[9]

Money is a tool. I believe 'unrighteous' here relates to something temporary and not something sinful. Jesus tells us to use our worldly resources to benefit others, so they will welcome us when we get to heaven. Other translations of these verses may help buttress this:

*And I say to you, Make friends for yourselves through the wealth of this life, so that when it comes to an end, you may be taken into the eternal resting-places (**Bible in Basic English**)*

*I tell you this. People may get money in wrong ways. But you should use it to be good to those who need help. You will die, one day. Then those people will be happy to see you in that place where people live for all time (**Easy English Version**)*

And I tell you, make friends for yourselves by how you use worldly wealth, so that when it runs out you will be welcomed into the eternal homes (New English Translation).

It's been said that money is like manure – in the sense that if you spread it all around, it makes things grow; but if you pile it up, it starts stinking. God wants us to use the temporary resources He has put in our hands as tools to do permanent good.

Verse eight has a way of tripping a lot of people off because they wonder why the dishonest man is being commended. But the point Jesus is making to his disciples (children of the Light) is this: If the 'children of this world' (who believe only in life here on earth) can be that shrewd about planning for their future which is short and temporary, why should they (who will live forever) be any less strategic in choosing how to use their resources to influence or secure their eternity?

Ultimately, what Jesus is telling us is that the best use of money is in getting people into heaven. God sees your money as a tool for populating heaven, not for lavishing on yourself. You may not take your money with you when you die, but you could send it ahead through those who are going there. Remember that Jesus said

"Do not lay up for yourselves treasures on earth..."[10]

He says to be careful and not be deceived into

stockpiling treasures for yourself on earth. Why?

- First, they may tarnish.
- Second, it can lose value. Your bank can even go-under (nowadays, it's no longer if but when).
- Third, someone may steal it.
- Finally, you can't take it with you when you die.

So, He says, why not rather store up your treasure where neither of these things would happen? Why not choose a place where your investment will appreciate and thieves can't break in? Where would that be? Heaven! How you do that is by using it to send people there. The reason Jesus gives this advice is that your heart always follows your money, and He doesn't want you to end up with a broken heart.

Also, in Apostle Paul's writing to Timothy (a young minister who was his protégé), he says:

"Command those who are rich in this world (present age) not to be haughty, nor to trust in uncertain riches but in the living God, who gives us richly all things to enjoy. Let them do good that they be rich in good works, ready to give, willing to share, storing up for themselves a good foundation for the time to come, that they may lay hold on eternal life."[11]

We see that both Jesus and Paul are saying the same thing, which is this: There is a connection between your money and eternity. The way you handle your money has eternal consequences. Make no mistake, money will not get you to heaven; accepting Jesus as your Saviour and following Him is how you get to heaven. If you do not have Jesus, it makes no difference how much money you give; you are going straight to hell. This is not about buying your way into heaven; but once you are saved, your generous giving becomes an investment in your eternal destiny.

Now imagine this: One day, you eventually die and make it to heaven. On your arrival at heaven's gate, there are hundreds or even thousands of people waiting at the entrance to receive you. They are clapping and cheering, saying, *"We've been waiting for you. We're so glad you're here. We are here because you spent your money to tell us the Good News. We are your friends for eternity because if it weren't for your generosity, we wouldn't have heard about how to get here."*

> Make no mistake, money will not get you to heaven; accepting Jesus as your Saviour and following Him is how you get to heaven.

So, are you using your money for this purpose? Is anybody going to be in heaven because of you, because of the way you use your money? Like I said earlier, you cannot take your money with you but you can send it on ahead. How? By investing in people who are going there. Each person you help hear the Good News, who accepts

Christ and goes to heaven, is an investment in your eternal Individual Retirement Account - an account that is awaiting you in heaven.

Principle 4: Money is a Test

The fourth principle is found in verses 10 to 12:

"He who is faithful in what is least is faithful also in much, and he who is unjust in what is least is unjust also in much. Therefore, if you have not been faithful in the unrighteous mammon, who will commit to your trust the true riches? And if you have not been faithful in what is another man's, who will give you what is your own?"[12]

God places a test before us using a variety of events and circumstances to expose the actual condition of our heart. Money is one of such tests.

Jesus says God sees your money as a test. In school, we expect a test at the end of a period; to drive a car, we go through a driving test; when we have a medical condition, a medical test may need to be conducted. The most important criteria we have comes from God. God places a test before us using a variety of events and circumstances to expose the actual condition of our heart. Money is one of such tests.

Faithfulness is a character attribute. If you have it, you will be faithful regardless of the quantity or size of what you have to manage.

Your money is a test –

one with rewards for today and tomorrow. If your money is a trust, then it is also a test. Notice that Jesus did not say he who is faithful in what is least would be faithful even in much. He says he who is faithful in little is faithful in much. Faithfulness is a character attribute. If you have it, you will be faithful regardless of the quantity or size of what you have to manage. One who is irresponsible with little is equally irresponsible with much.

This principle applies to every area of life. In fact, you could say this is the best career advice in the Bible. Faithfulness, in little ways, produces fruitfulness in significant ways. You say, *"When I make it big, then I'll really become generous."* No, you won't! There is no correlation between being successful and being generous. Successful people are successful and generous people are generous, period.

> There is no correlation between being successful and being generous.

If you manage well what God gave you, then God will trust you with more.

"To those who use well what they are given, even more, will be given, and they will have an abundance. But from those who do nothing, even what little they have will be taken away."[13]

As you manage what God has given you in the way He

tells you to, you will have abundance in every area of your life.

Principle 5:
Money is a Revealer

Finally, in verse 15 of our reference text, Jesus says the way you handle money is an identity issue:

"No servant can serve two masters; for either he will hate the one and love the other, or else he will be loyal to the one and despise the other. You cannot serve God and mammon."[14]

Jesus says your money is a revealer. Your view of money, the way you handle it and what money can buy, reveals who is king over your heart. For many Christians, Jesus is their Saviour but He is not yet their Lord.

The place of money in your heart remains the best indicator of who your lord really is. It is either God or money - there is no middle ground. You may not have thought about it this way, but it's true. Jesus says money is the only thing that has the power to compete with God for the throne of your heart.

So, the question is: Whose are you? The answer lies in your bank chequebook stubs or statement of account.

Chapter Two

THE TITHE QUESTION

"Do you use to make ends meet by stealing?
No more! Get an honest job so that you can
help others who can't work."

– Apostle Paul

The Tithe Question

Most people make the error of viewing a concept of the Bible in isolation of the grand narrative of scripture. They miss the distinction between purpose and practice and confuse principles with applications. It is often this parochial view that leads to unnecessary debate or arguments about what is Old or New Testament.

Take the whole brouhaha about tithing, for instance. Proponents on both sides of the divide seem satisfied with just quoting a few verses of scripture here and there to buttress their point of view; but the Bible was not given to us for the purpose of arguments and debates. The Bible is to help us discern the mind of God. Throwing around snippets of scriptures without connecting the dots throughout the Bible will leave us with a faulty theology.

Let me say this upfront: I believe that we may well determine the applicability of tithing by one's theological approach, rather than by exegesis – a critical explanation of isolated scriptures alone. That

> Throwing around snippets of scriptures without connecting the dots throughout the Bible will leave us with a faulty theology.

said, lets continue.

As you may already know, the Bible comprises many little stories, genres, and narratives pointing in one direction. These narratives can be broadly classified into four movements: The creation, the fall, redemption, and the new creation.

From the beginning, God's primary intent and purposes have spanned the entire spectrum of these movements and they have never changed. Practices may have changed and methods revised or abandoned; but the purposes and principles of God have not changed.

The big question is: Why the tithe(s)? What was the broad purpose even in the Old Testament? The answer to these questions may give us an insight into the relevance of the practice regardless of the dispensation. We cannot talk about tithing without looking at the classic biblical text on tithing.

"Will a man rob God? Yet you have robbed me! But you say, 'In what way have we robbed you?' In tithes and offerings. You are cursed with a curse, for you have robbed Me, even this nation. Bring all the tithes into the storehouse, that there may be food in My house and try Me now in this," says the Lord of Hosts, "If I will not open for you the windows of heaven and pour out for you such blessing that there will be no room enough to receive it."[1].

God is asking, "Will a man rob God?" The word 'rob' (as used here) doesn't have the same meaning as taking what is not yours illegally or by force. In its root in the Hebrew, this is a powerful word that appears in only two places in the Bible. It means to plunder or pillage and oppress.

The picture or illustration that comes to mind is that of a powerful nation over-running a smaller and weaker country. That is why in this imaginary dialogue that God was having with His people, He expected them to be shocked – and they were. They wondered how on earth mere mortals could rob God. So they ask, *"…in what way are we doing that to you?"* And God replies, *"…in tithes and offerings."*

From these verses, first, we need to understand that God did not imply that His people were plundering Him directly. Second, from God's point of view, there is more to it than just withholding generosity or being stingy. God was referring to something much vaster.

To know God's mind, we have to unearth His values in creation; we have to go back to the beginning. In Genesis, we see that God was in a loving relationship and partnership in the Godhead before He created man. Their relationship is characterized by mutual giving, honouring and glorifying of one another. When God created man, He also wanted a similar relationship for him. He went to a great extent preparing an elaborate garden – a place of beauty, harmony, and peace. Then, He created Eve – a helper. God planned that both of them (in a loving, giving and serving partnership) will work together and be productive (as in the Godhead). The reward for their work will benefit their relationship and also replenish the earth. The proceeds of their work will be for the mutual benefit and good of all. This way, the world will remain a place of interconnecting beauty, love and peace, where all of mankind can flourish.

So when God gave man abilities, aptitude, strength, and opportunities that lead to increase, He expected that some of that increase would be ploughed back into the human community for the common good of all and for the security and sustenance of His creation. A person is only truly as wealthy and healthy as his community. Therefore, a man's dignity is connected to his contribution.

Work offers humanity a vehicle for sharing and exchange and there lies the dignity of labour. God didn't give Adam work in the garden for the purpose of earning a living. He fully provided everything Adam needed even before he was created hence, Adam's work was for dignity; it was his means of contributing to the flourishing of humanity. Let's look at the mind of God in the following scripture:

> *A person is only truly as wealthy and healthy as his community. Therefore, a man's dignity is connected to his contribution.*

"Anyone who has been stealing must steal no longer, but must work, doing something useful with their own hands, that they may have something to share with those in need."[2]

Therefore, the end purpose of work is to contribute towards the good of all. Hence, when this is not the motive of God's people, God says their action is equivalent to disintegrating, dismantling and defrauding His creation.

God's mind has always been about love and generous sharing. His intention when He

> *God didn't give Adam work in the garden for the purpose of earning a living. He fully provided everything Adam needed even before he was created*

created us was for us to be free. He wanted us to be unashamed and unencumbered so that we could have strong, intimate relationship with Him and with one another. Satan tempted Adam (mankind), and he fell into sin by disobeying and breaking trust with God. From then on, man lost his freedom and chose slavery. God made us for freedom, but sin made us slaves.

One of the greatest misfortunes of sin and man's sinful nature after his fall was that man developed an unhealthy relationship with his possessions. He gained a propensity to hoard and be selfish. To restore and promote His values among His chosen nation, Israel, as an example to the rest of humanity and a foreshadow of what's coming in Christ, God decided that all of His people should live within a margin. This was (and still is) one of the primary purposes of the tithe. The 'Law of the Tithe' in the Old Testament (like the 'Gleaning Rule' or 'Rule of the harvest') served many purposes from God's perspective. First, let's talk about the Gleaning Rule.

The economy of ancient Israel was primarily agricultural. This was especially true in biblical times. The Bible is replete with passages on sowing, reaping, threshing, and milling. The annual harvest of grains, olives, and grapes represented a significant portion, if not the majority, of the national economic production. Besides playing a vital role in the national economy, grain was an essential dietary

> One of the greatest misfortunes of sin and man's sinful nature after his fall was that man developed an unhealthy relationship with his possessions.

staple that plays a critical role in people's everyday lives. The instructions God gave to Moses for the Israelites captures this rule:

"When you reap the harvest of your land, do not reap to the edges of your field or gather the gleanings of your harvest. Do not go over your vineyard a second time or pick up the grapes that have fallen. Leave them for the poor and for the foreigner. I am the Lord your God."[3]

You will find a repeat of this commandment in Leviticus 23:22. Forty years later, Moses characteristically expands on the command in Deuteronomy 24:19-21. The people are not to harvest to the edge of their fields, nor go over the ground a second time to pick up leftovers after the harvesters had bundled the sheaves of grain. In the same way, he prohibited the Israelites from beating their olive trees a second time or returning to recover what fruit remained after picking the vine. According to Moses, God gave this instruction to provide sustenance for people who lived on society's margins. It was to serve as a social protection system (or a social safety net if you like), to take care of the weak and vulnerable; people with little or no means of substance, including the Levites and the Priests as can be seen in Deuteronomy 14:28-29; 26:12. This was part of God's plan to ensure that no Israelite, not even strangers amongst them, ever have to live in abject poverty.

This rule saved Naomi and Ruth when they returned to Israel broke and without a breadwinner. The book of Ruth provides an instructive example of how this worked. One of the book's significant protagonists, Ruth, is both a widow and a foreigner and the other was Naomi, her mother-in-law who was also a widow. Both of them returned to Bethlehem of Judah from Moab in penury; this generosity system sustained them.

Taking a look at the Tithing Rules, let's review the types of tithes and their purposes. A tithe is one-tenth part of something paid as a contribution to a religious organization or as a compulsory tax to the government. The Levitical law prescribed it thus:

"And all the tithe of the land whether of the seed of the land or of the fruit of the tree, is the LORD's. It is holy to the LORD. If a man wants at all to redeem any of his tithes, he shall add one-fifth to it. And concerning the tithe of the herds or the flock, of whatever passes under the rod, the tenth one shall be holy to the LORD."[4]

In the Old Testament, the law required a minimum of three kinds of tithes:

1. The Levite Tithe (maaserrishon)

"I give to the Levites all the tithes in Israel as their inheritance in return for the work they do while serving at the tent meeting."[5]

This tithe was compensation to the tribe of Levi because they didn't receive a landed inheritance in the promise land. Therefore, to support them while performing their duties at the tent of meeting and subsequently the temple and other services within the communities, the rest of the tribes were to give them a tithe of their harvest.

What if I told you that the Priests and Levites did more than just serve in the temple? Most Levites were the professionals of their days. Here are a few of the other duties they performed:

- They were ordained to be teachers of the nation (Deuteronomy 24:8; 33:10; 2 Chronicles 35:3; Nehemiah 8:7).

- They serve as judges of the land and in the time of Ezra, they were the sole members of the Sanhedrin – the Supreme Court of the nation (Deuteronomy 17:8-9, 21:5; 1 Chronicles 23:4; 2 Chronicles 19:8; Ezekiel 44:15,24).

- Most medical services within the communities were provided by the Levites (Leviticus 13:2; 14:2, Luke 17:14).

- They were professional singers and musicians (1 Chronicle 25:1-31; 2 Chronicles 5:12; 34:12).

- The Levites almost exclusively produced books and served as librarians (2 Chronicles 34:13).

- Hard to believe, but they even served as law enforcement officers (1 Chronicles 23:4)
- Many of the Levites were architects and builders (2 Chronicles 34:8-13)

The Levite Tithe (gift) was given on produce not in cash – even though there was a legal currency in circulation in Israel – and it was not used for the maintenance of the tabernacle of meeting or the temple. The temple was maintained by a tax (Temple tax) of a fixed amount (half a shekel) to be paid by all Israelites.

This tithe is no longer valid for at least two reasons:

Firstly, all of us are now heir according to promise (Galatians 3:29) but more than heirs, all who believe in Christ are joint heirs with Jesus.

"The Spirit Himself bears witness with our spirit that we are children of God, and if children, then heirs – heirs of God and joint heirs with Christ, if indeed we have suffered with Him, that we may also be glorified together."[6]

No one is disenfranchised. We all have access collectively and individually to the provisions and promises secured through the cross of Christ.

Secondly, the Levitical priesthood has been abolished in the New Testament. Jesus has fulfilled the law and has ended all temple worship. He has made us saints (priests and kings) blessed with spiritual gifts and called to do the work of ministry. Even in Judaism, this tithe has no meaning today.

To acknowledge this reality as a believer and at the same time, try to draw the benefits associated with an abolished system (Hebrew 7:1-22) is mischievous at the very least.

There is a critical issue of ministerial remuneration. How should Pastors be catered for in the New Testament? This is important because I suspect that those who oppose the concept of tithing do so more out of displeasure and frustration with the way the proceeds are administered and applied by church leaders. We will discuss this question momentarily; but in the meantime, let's continue with types of tithes and their relevance today.

2. The Second Tithe (maasersheni) is a Tithe for Feasts.

"Be sure to set aside a tenth of all that your fields produce each year. Eat the tithe of your grain, new wine and olive oil, and the firstborn of your herds and flocks in the presence of the Lord your God at the place he will choose as a dwelling for his Name."[7]

This is a tithe for the feasts to be taken to Jerusalem. It was a tithe to the good of man himself, for a vacation and specifically, a holiday with a religious purpose.

The Levitical law required that Jews had to go up to Jerusalem on certain occasions like the feasts of Passover, Pentecost and Tabernacles. In reality, this sacred ordinance included a definite social provision – periods of vacation for the family. And how should the head of the household provide for the vacation expenses? By setting aside a second tithe. This tithe can be redeemed by substituting for it with a sum of money, which is then taken to Jerusalem and used for the purchase of food and drink to be consumed there.

So, this was more like a compulsory saving plan. Saving, of course, remains a relevant and necessary financial management tool. But as a religious requirement, this tithe is also no longer valid; those feasts have all been fulfilled in the New Testament. Therefore, the Scriptures do not demand that we perform any pilgrimage to Jerusalem as believers in Christ.

3. The Third Tithe (maaserani) is the Tithe for the Poor

"At the end of every third year you shall bring out the tithe of your produce within the year and store it up within your gates. And the Levite, because he has no portion nor inheritance with you, and the stranger and the fatherless and the widow who are within your gates, may come and eat and be satisfied, that the Lord your God may bless you in all the work of your hand which you do."[8]

This tithe was given every third year specifically for charity and communal fellowship. What that means is that this tithe is a third of all the tithes over a six-year period.

This is the only tithe that is still relevant today and perhaps dearest to God's heart. Many scriptural verses support giving to charity both in the Old and New Testament.

God's focus has always been on community rather than on individual prosperity - a commonwealth.

All across the Bible, God's focus has always been on community rather than on individual prosperity - a commonwealth. Many of the promises in the Bible (that we so quickly claim for ourselves as individuals) were promises made to a people – not to a person. The first-century Church understood and practiced this principle because Jesus pushed it relentlessly. Hence, the early disciples sold their landed properties to create a commonwealth in their communities and amplified the message of Jesus. And as a result,

"Now the multitude of those who believed were of one heart and one soul; neither did anyone say that any of the things he possessed was his own, but they had all things in common. And with great power the Apostles gave witness to the resurrection of the Lord Jesus. And great grace was upon them all. Nor was there anyone among them who lacked; for all who were possessors of land or houses sold them, and brought the proceeds of the things that were

sold, and laid them at the Apostles feet; and they distributed to each as anyone had need."9

So, how should we view tithing in the New Testament? That's perhaps the hottest debate within and maybe even outside the Christian community in Nigeria and around the world today.

Several arguments to support tithing have stressed the obligatory requirements. As I mentioned earlier, Christ abolished the legal requirements of the old covenants because He is the end of the law and the temple. Jesus said, *"kill me and in three days, not only this temple, but all other temples in the world will be out of business."* (paraphrased) – and that was what happened.

In the New Testament, our focus is on the grace of God. The writer of Hebrews gives a basic instruction:

*"See to it that no one misses the grace of God."*10

When we experience grace, we no longer live to appease (pacify, palliate, allay) God but to give Him pleasure.

See that no one fails to experience the grace of God. That is so powerful because when we experience grace, we no longer live to appease (pacify, palliate, allay) God but to give Him pleasure. Grace, by definition, implies that something is undeserved, and an expression of 'thanks' would be reasonable and natural. Thanks and Grace could be regarded as interchangeable. That is why some people might describe the blessing of a meal or the offering of thanks before a meal as 'saying the grace'. To 'say grace' means you understand 'thanks'. They go together.

I feel those who really understand the nature of God's grace and the devastating reality of their unworthiness are more easily overwhelmed with life-changing gratitude. They know that everything they have, they have received (1 Corinthians 4:7). So, there is a direct relationship between grace and gratitude. A grateful heart is a generous heart. When we are grateful, our generous giving is no longer motivated by the fear of a curse or an obligation of faith or even the desire for a reward, but by the sheer desire to please God and give Him pleasure.

> When we are grateful, our generous giving is no longer motivated by the fear of a curse or an obligation of faith or even the desire for a reward, but by the sheer desire to please God and give Him pleasure.

In the New Testament, Jesus referred to tithing only once in the gospels

"Woe to you scribes and Pharisees, hypocrites! For you pay tithe of mint and cumin and have neglected the weightier matters of the law: justice and mercy and faith. These you ought to have done, without leaving the others undone."[11]

This is a brief, yet, essential reference. Let me paraphrase the text in my own words:

"You tithe everything to the last piece of spice in your kitchen. But once you've done that, you feel that you have fulfilled all your obligations and owe no one anything else. You won't help anyone again even when justice and grace demand you do so. You are mere legalists who are not motivated by love."

To get Jesus' point here, you must bear this one crucial thing in mind: From the beginning, when Jesus launched His ministry, He (more or less) drew a line in the sand. Right out of His first sermon, popularly referred to as 'The Sermon on the Mount', His mission was to reset the peoples' standards for relating with God and, upturn some of the theology of His days. Jesus raised the bar on the standards of the Old Testament. He raised the bar on marital fidelity, generosity, vengeance and many more. He gradually laid down a marker for what would come and what He was about to introduce. In this brief reference to the tithe, Jesus sounded a warning to the Pharisees and everyone else that 90% was not absolutely theirs to keep even after paying the tithes, but they must go beyond the tithe when justice and mercy and love demands it; because the whole 100% (not just 10%) belongs to God. This is not the only place where Jesus sent a signal that the grand old order was changing.

"Now Jesus sat opposite the treasury and saw how the

people put money into the treasury. And many who were rich put in much. Then one poor widow came and threw in two mites, which make a quadrans. So He called His disciples to Himself and said to them, Assuredly, I say to you that this poor widow has put in more than all those you have given to the treasury; for they all put in out of their abundance, but she out of her poverty put in all that she had, her whole livelihood."[12] (Emphasis mine)

Again in these verses, Jesus shows us, in an object lesson to the disciples, what would characterize New Testament generosity. There is no doubt in my mind that the Apostles got His message because when the Church began in the first century, they put no pressure or demand on the new converts; yet, many sold their belongings and created an everyday purse from where the needy were catered for.

Now, let's briefly fast-forward to the era of the ministry of Apostle Paul. In the first century, there was famine in Judah and the church in Jerusalem was feeling the pinch. Apostle Paul was moved to do something about it so he wrote letters to the Gentile churches to which he had oversight, asking them to raise an offering for relief to the saints in Jerusalem.

Paul was a thoroughbred Pharisee before he became a follower of Jesus. He would have known about tithing and may have been a faithful practitioner. So, this audacious project would have been a perfect opportunity to introduce it to the Gentile churches; but he didn't! As a matter of fact, no New Testament writer either encouraged 'tithing' or presented it as the normative or even occasional practice of the Church.

Rather than a *"flash the tithe card"*, Apostle Paul focuses on grace and the gospel of our Lord Jesus. In 2 Corinthians 8, Paul shares the testimony of the Macedonian church as an example for the church in Corinth to emulate. The Bible says they gave themselves first to God before giving their monies. They gave willingly, gladly and sacrificially, urging the disciples (who were reluctant to take from them because of their meagre means) to receive their generosity.

In challenging the church in Corinth to follow in the footsteps of the Macedonian Church, we see that Paul did not put pressure on the will of the people. *"I am not commanding you..."*[13] he said. He also did not put pressure on their emotions neither did he use guilt or fear. Instead, he pointed them to the cross. Paul gives them the Jesus-standard - the standard that Jesus alluded to in Matthew 23 and Mark 12 above.

> 10% is no longer the giving standard for a New Testament believer , the cross of Jesus Christ is the new standard for measuring generosity.

10% is no longer the giving standard for a New Testament believer and this is why the Apostles did not talk about tithe in the New Testament. The cross of Jesus Christ is the new standard for measuring generosity. Jesus, like the widow in Mark 12, gave all; He gave sacrificially. According to Pastor Tim Keller the founding Pastor of Redeemer Presbyterian Church, New York, imagine if Jesus gave a tithe of His blood, we would still be lost. When we see it from this point of view, 10% becomes a pitiful response to the extravagant love of God towards us.

Here are fundamental New Testament principles through which we must filter our giving:

- If your generosity doesn't compel you to adjust or reign in your luxurious lifestyle, then there is no 'Cross' in it. You are giving out of your surplus; therefore, there is no sacrifice.

- If your giving (or by whatever name you choose to call it) is not motivated by the Cross, it's not Christ-centred and not the gospel.

- It is irresponsible for any community of faith to permit abject poverty especially one that collects tithe. Apostle James defined abject poverty in the Scriptures thus: *"Suppose a brother or sister is without clothes and daily food. If one of you says to them, "Go in peace; keep warm and well-fed", but does nothing about their physical needs,*

Focusing on the term 'tithe' alone, is a huge distraction from the whole concept of a selfless life of generosity.

what good is it?"[14]

Let me quickly point out that focusing on the term 'tithe' alone, is a huge distraction from the whole concept of a selfless life of generosity.

Now, let's go back to the question of remuneration for church leaders. Without income from obligatory giving (tithe), how should the churches care for their leaders?

Two things are obvious in the New Testament about this question: the first is that the Bible has a lot to say on this subject and the second is that there is no connection between the care for Pastors and tithing.

"Don't you know that those who serve in the temple get their food from the temple, and those who serve at the altar share in what is offered on the altar? In the same way, the Lord has commanded that those who preach the gospel should receive their living from the gospel."[15]

In these verses and the subsequent below, Apostle Paul affirms that the ministers of God's Work should be cared for in the New Testament just as they were in the Old Testament. Paul and Barnabas chose to work and support themselves rather than rely on the church because they did not want to be accused of preaching for money.

"The elders who direct the affairs of the church well are worthy of double honour, especially those whose work is preaching and teaching. For scripture says, "Do not

muzzle an ox while it is treading out grain," and a worker deserves his wages."[16]

"Nevertheless, one who receives instruction in the word should share all good things with their instructor."[17]

These verses reiterate the fact that a minister of the gospel should be well remunerated. It is an ordinance of God. Yet, we cannot deny that there are excesses. So, what should be the guide? Here's a thought to ponder on (from a respected theologian).

*"St. Paul contends that a preacher of the Gospel has a right to his support; and he has proved this from the **law**, from the **Gospel**, and from the **common sense** and consent of men. If a man who does not labour takes his maintenance from the Church of God, it is not only a domestic theft, but a sacrilege. He that gives up his time to this labour has a right to the support of himself and family; he who takes more than is sufficient for this purpose is a covetous hireling. He who does nothing for the cause of God and religion and yet obliges the church to support him and minister to his idleness, irregularities, luxury, avarice, and ambition, is a monster for whom human language has not yet got a name."[18]*

So why do church leaders still insist on a tithe? A number of reasons but I think the most rational reason arise from the fear that people will no longer support the work of ministry financially if they are not obliged to. In the mind of these leaders, the fear of been plagued with a curse if members refuse to tithe has helped to keep many of their congregants faithful. Therefore, removing this constrain will certainly spell doom for their churches financially.

On the contrary, I honestly believe that if people are taught to be generous and pointed to the cross of Christ, they will give more and do so with cheerful exuberance. If money is a medium of exchange then how poorly it compares to the most powerful medium of exchange on the earth – the cross?

Chapter Three

YOUR MONEY AND GREED

"There is enough in the world for everyone's need, but not enough for everyone's greed."

Frank Buchman (1871 - 1961)
Protestant Christian Evangelist

Your Money And Greed

It is hard to deny that capitalism is the best economic system around. It creates wealth far better than feudalism, communism, socialism or any other system one could name. But for all its advantages, capitalism has a major drawback that kingdom people need to worry about; it requires people to stay perpetually hungry for more. Capitalism runs on greed and materialism, but God has an answer to that.

God says, pick a percentage of your income and live on it. Now, whether you consciously decide on the percentage you will live on or not, we all ultimately live on a percentage. For some, it's 80% or less, for some others, 90%, 100%, 120% or more. Why not be deliberate? Why not be proactive? It will give you control over your money; otherwise, your money will control you and eventually undermine your happiness.

Therefore, as a lifestyle, create a margin for generosity. Recall that we talked earlier about the gleaning rule and the tithe in ancient Israel and how it provided a safety net for the vulnerable in the society. Aside that, I believe it was also God's way of developing in His people a lifestyle of generosity and a buffer against the disease of greed.

God gave the Israelites tithing as an integral part of their stewardship system to check greed. Greed is cancer that eats away at your spiritual bones. What makes greed so dangerous is that it is the most subtle of the seven deadly sins. It is so insidious that those who have it are unaware they do. It is something you notice in other people but never recognize in your own life– because greed cannot be seen in the mirror.

Jesus tells us, in Matthew 6:22 that greed and materialism is a sin of the eye – it blinds you to its presence. No wonder He says to watch out for greed. In Luke 12:15, Jesus warns that we should be on guard against all kinds of greed and materialism because a man's life does not consist of the abundance of the things, which he possesses. Why would He ask us to watch out and be on guard? It is because greed hides. You might be greedy and not know it. Now, if you go

> Greed is cancer that eats away at your spiritual bones.

"Not me! Me, greedy? Na!" That's a terrible sign! If you are committing any other sin, you will know it. You can't be committing adultery and not know it. But greed? It is always any other person but you - your rich uncle, the renowned politician, or the famous businessman across town.

In my years as a pastor, people have come for counsel on several areas of struggle. Many have freely spoken about their addictions and challenges with drugs, sex, anger, pride or gambling; but no one has ever come to confess the sin of greed or materialism. No one has ever said: *"You know, pastor, I think I am greedy. I need help."*

You can see why the Bible talks relentlessly about greed. Preachers are quick to point to how often Jesus preached about money, to justify why they need to talk about money all the time. The question is, what exactly was Jesus' focus in His parables and teachings on money? His primary focus was on how to relate to money and wealth. I have heard people make arguments in favour of greed. Their point being that greed can be useful when it motivates us to do our best to serve others to the best of our ability and then get the rewards that come with it (money, recognition, status, etc.). This is the way the world thinks; and it is what is being promoted everywhere you turn – movies, television, school, work or even board games like Monopoly or Game of Life – the person who ends up with the most stuff is always the winner.

Greed is the ideology suited to our dumbed-down consumer culture, and it's what our society encourages and rewards. Listen to Gordon Gekko, in the film Wall Street (1987):

"Greed, for the lack of a better word, is good. Greed is right, greed works. Greed clarifies, cuts through, and captures the essence of the evolutionary spirit. Greed, in all of its forms - greed for life, for money, for love, knowledge - has marked the upward surge of mankind."

That's the voice of someone embarrassed by his greed but hides it behind a great excuse and a carefully crafted persona. Even if we permit ourselves the mistake of ever thinking greed may be useful for economies, it is not suitable for the individual. A person who is consumed by greed becomes utterly fixated on the object of his desire. He reduces life to a little more than a quest to accumulate and hoard as much as possible of whatever he craves. To think of greed as a virtue in any form is to miss the whole point. Greed is unreasonable.

By overcoming reason, compassion and love, greed undoes family and community ties and undermines the values on which we build our society and civilization. Greed may fuel the economy, but (as recent history has made all too clear) it almost always leads us into a deeper, more painful and long-lasting economic problems.

A person who is consumed by greed becomes utterly fixated on the object of his desire.

Ultimately, greed is not really about money or things; it is just a symptom or pointer to a deeper issue. The issue is not about quantity but a condition of the heart. Greed is really a way of dealing with our own feelings of deficit and emptiness. It's not so much about having enough, but about being enough. When we lose faith in God and belief in ourselves; when we feel we are not enough, then we get greedy. We try to use things to fill the hole inside us. Greed is an appetite. Horace, the ancient Roman Poet said, *"He who is greedy is always in want."* The desire for money and stuff is an appetite that can never be fully and completely satisfied. It is a bottomless pit that keeps asking for more but never gets filled. It deceives and convinces us that if we have a little more... then we'll be... (Fill in the blanks with whatever it might be for you). This is the "if" and "then" myth. For example: *If I have more money, then I will be happy, or I would have a more secure future.*

> Greed is really a way of dealing with our own feelings of deficit and emptiness. It's not so much about having enough, but about being enough. When we lose faith in God and belief in ourselves; when we feel we are not enough, then we get greedy.

The real issue, however, is fear – the fear of lack. The fear of the lack of money is the real definition of poverty. Real poverty is not the lack of money because you can have a lot of money and still be poor. The state of being poor is when we allow fear of the lack of money to dominate you. It is a scarcity mentality that leads to an intense focus on self-preservation, and self-preservation always leads to hoarding which expresses itself in greed.

You may be familiar with some basic version of the Greek myth of Narcissus, the extremely beautiful youth who falls in love with himself after seeing his reflection in a pool of water. Afraid that he would lose sight of his image, he stayed right at the edge of the pool till he died of starvation. What was he starving for? Something he already possessed. He didn't know it. That is how greed works. Too many of us perish on the edge of our societal reflecting pool, pining for images of ourselves that are fitter, richer, sexier, and smarter. By our greed and self-absorption, we starve ourselves of the happiness, joy, and well-being we could experience at the moment.

Think about it for a moment, how much money do you need to be happy or completely satisfied and content? Fifty million? One hundred million? What about one billion? The answer is the same for all of us: More than you currently have. After responding to the man who was seeking His intervention in an inheritance dispute that led to the warning about greed in Luke 12, Jesus illustrated His point with a parable popularly called the Parable of the Rich Fool.

"Then He spoke a parable to them, saying: the ground of a certain rich man yielded plentifully. And he thought

*within himself, saying, 'what shall I do since I have no room to store my crops?' So he said 'I will do this: I will pull down my barns and build greater, and there I will store all my crops and my goods. And I will say to my soul, "Soul, you have many goods laid up for many years; take ease; eat, drink, and be merry." But God said to him, 'Fool! This night your soul will be required of you; then whose will those things be which you have provided? So is he who lays up treasure for himself, and not **rich** toward God."[1]* (emphasis, mine)

Greed uses external things to deal with internal matters–and it never works. It leaves us wanting more. Greed shows us to be living in poverty towards God. The antidote then is to be rich towards God, and being rich towards God begins with knowing we already are God's precious treasures. He treasures us sacrificially. He died to make us His treasures; whereas all other treasures demand we die to have them (and that's why some people work themselves to the bones for their careers, or possessions, or even for love). Jesus is the only treasure who died to make you His treasure.

It's often said, *"temptation commonly comes through that for which we are naturally fitted."* If a man is fitted to handle money, temptation comes for him to regard money as the most important thing in the world. Judas was evidently a gifted Accountant – perhaps that was why he was chosen to take care of the treasury; but he became so fond of money that he became a thief. See how he interprets a genuine display of love by Mary:

"Then Mary took a pound of very costly oil of spikenard, anointed the feet of Jesus, and wiped His feet with her hair. And the house was filled with the fragrance of the oil. But one of the disciples, Judas Iscariot, Simon's son, who would betray Him, said, "Why was this fragrance oil not sold for three hundred denarii and given to the poor?" This he said, not because he cared for the poor, but because he was a thief, and had the money box; and used to take what was put in it."[2]

He couldn't see Mary's act of worship as an expression of surpassing love; rather, he saw it as a waste. A man's sight depends on the condition of his heart. Jesus said,

"The lamp of the body is the eye. If therefore your eye is good, your whole body will be full of light. But if your eye is bad, your whole body will be full of darkness. If therefore the light that is in you is darkness, how great is that darkness."[3]

The question is, why would Jesus, who knew exactly who Judas was, permit him to manage the ministry's purse? I believe Jesus was putting His money where his mouth was. Judas helped prove that Jesus' advice was infallible. In the preceding verses, He said,

"Do not lay up treasures on earth, where thieves break in and steal... Where your treasure is, there your heart will be also."[4]

The end of Judas exposes the heart-hardening, heart-blinding, heart-breaking end of someone corrupted by greed. Greed begins with awareness (which starts the moment you know what the other has, or what there is to have that you don't have). Advertisers know this. Their job is to make you aware and create discontent for what you already have, or for what you can have but don't have yet. If you fall for the bait, you're trapped! Your desires become warped. Apostle Paul calls them "foolish and harmful" desires in 1 Timothy 6 – because it's a deception! I have nothing against advertising, but have you noticed that today's adverts no longer promote the quality and value of a product, but now it's all about lifestyles? They take a good thing of real value (like love, friendship or belonging) and tell you that you can have one or all of that if you buy their product. The goal is to make you feel that a particular product will give you pleasure and make you happy. But you know this, don't you? It won't! It's a lie! While a product may bring you momentary pleasure, hardly does any product bring lasting happiness. Yet, it doesn't stop you from moving from one product to another, thinking each new one will bring you the happiness you seek. How often have we confused pleasure with happiness? The two are not the same. Happiness can bring you

> Greed begins with awareness (which starts the moment you know what the other has, or what there is to have that you don't have).

pleasure, but not all pleasure brings happiness. Many a pleasure may undermine your goal of lasting happiness. Therefore, it is awareness that drives appetite, and an unsatisfied appetite fuels discontentment.

"Hope deferred makes the heart sick."[5]

You are never satisfied with what you have because you know of what others have and what there is to have. This makes greed addictive; and the more you feed it, the more it grows. Greed never travels alone; other vices like jealousy, envy, and stinginess accompany it. To be honest, I suspect that some of the venom and tirade in the exchanges on the tithing subject is not unconnected with greed and jealousy on both sides of the divide.

Social media has made matters worse. Reviewing posts by 'friends' on Instagram or Facebook has made comparison a daily or even an hourly affair. Even though those posts are merely the highlight reels of another person's life, we are not spared the agony of comparison. It is so simple: When you get a little money, you can buy things you couldn't afford in the past – and that feels good. Suddenly, you cannot live without the things you once used to live without well enough. Before long, your wants become needs, and luxuries turn into necessities. The one thing everyone wants to have (or think they need) is this one word right here: More! We often say it to others or ourselves, don't we? "If only I can have just a little more of…"

"Those who love money (devoted or have a strong attachment to it) never have enough, those who love wealth are never satisfied with their income."[6] (The words in bracket are mine.)

Culture baits us to think that we can never really be happy unless we get more; because the more money we have, the happier and more enjoyable our lives would be. What this means is that money is not really our ultimate desire or pursuit; our real goal is happiness. Sadly, many have it all mixed up; they make the pursuit of money their end game rather than a means to an end.

You probably know many people who have more than enough money to make them happy; yet, they are still not happy, and others who struggle financially; yet, are happier. For many, it isn't more money that's needed. If you would permit yourself a thorough audit of your finances over any reasonable length of time, you are most likely to be amazed at how much money has passed through your hands over the period. Frankly, we need no more money

> Money is not really our ultimate desire or pursuit; our real goal is happiness.

> If you would permit yourself a thorough audit of your finances over any reasonable length of time, you are most likely to be amazed at how much money has passed through your hands over the period.

than we need better management.

Money and happiness connect around the word–manage! It is not how much money you have, but how well you manage what you have that determines whether you will be happy when it comes to money. If you mismanage your money, you will undermine your own peace regardless of how much money you earn. If you do not manage your money correctly, your money will manage you. And if you allow your money to manipulate you, you will be out of control and lose your peace.

> It is not how much money you have, but how well you manage what you have that determines whether you will be happy when it comes to money.

Jesus showed us in Luke 16 (which we discussed in chapter one) that, God owns; we manage. Problems begin when we decide to own and refuse to manage. 'Managing money' means getting a handle on how money works and being disciplined enough to create financial margins.

DEBTS

Greed always eventually leads to the ultimate predictable outcome of a life devoted to 'more' – Debts! Debt (consumer debts in particular) is a clear indicator that you have become a slave to your desires. Debt is one easy way through which greed takes control of the reins of your life.

"The rich rule over the poor, and the borrower is slave to the lender."[7]

The lender, instead of God, becomes your master. He dictates what you can have and what you cannot. He wants to be paid first. He closes the door on your ability to be generous and overrules God's instructions on stewardship.

According to Nathan Morris, the English Evangelist known for the Bay Revival, anytime you borrow money, you're robbing your future self. Debt is a trap! There is something about debt that tempts you to keep spending even when you can't afford the payment. It's greed! Part of the allure of debt is the fact that you can get an emotional high from getting a new thing now, without having to deal with the pain of parting with the money immediately. It can feel like getting something for nothing until it's time to pay up. Even the happiest of people can find the pressure and embarrassment of debts too much to handle.

Dr. John Gathergood of the University of Nottingham studied the correlation between carrying debt and depression and anxiety. In that study, Gathergood found that those who struggle to pay off their debts and loans are more than twice as likely to experience a host of mental health problems, including depression and severe anxiety. Debt and stress go hand-in-hand. In fact, arguments about money are top predictor of divorce – according to Sonya Britt, Assistant Professor of Family Studies at Kansas State University.

The press can be relentless, it starts with emails and telephone calls from creditors at all hours of the day and night. It is an unfortunate fact that sometimes, those suffering from these kinds of intense pressure become depressed or even attempt suicide. As you can see, debt can have direct impact on a person's life. It sometimes starts out as a good thing, allowing you to live the life you may otherwise be unable to live, but it ends up taking control and negatively influencing your life. Do everything possible to avoid debts and do not let it ruin your happiness.

It is incredible that the church, rather than teach people never to get into debts and educate those who are already in it to get out, would organize prayer meetings for debt cancellation and prophesy debt forgiveness. The truth is, God is on the side of the creditor. If you are a disciple of Jesus, you must pay what you owe. That's what the Bible says – and that's what God expects.

"The wicked borrows but does not pay back, but the righteous is generous and gives."[8]

If you are already in debts, while I pray for God to open new doors of financial opportunities to you, I will recommend that you seek help on how to budget and manage your income.

Chapter Four

GOD'S PLAN

"I know the plans I have for you," declares the Lord, "Plans to prosper you and not to harm you, plans to give you hope and a future."

Prophet Jeremiah

God's Plan

A Tale of Two Houses

It's amazing the difference a good plan can make. The Winchester Mystery House is one of the most popular tourist attractions in San Jose, California. Built by Sarah Winchester, heiress to the Winchester Rifle fortune, the house is huge (with more than 116 rooms).

But people do not visit the house because it is beautiful; they visit because it's weird.

Winchester built her home over the course of 32 years. From the time she started in 1884 until her death in 1922, she never stopped constructing. For the most part, she made things up as she went along. She built her home without a plan and because there was no plan, the house has a lot of odd features. There are rooms with no entrances, stairways leading nowhere, windows in floors and doors that open to nothing. The house is big, but it's a big mess. It's unsafe, confusing and full of wasted potentials.

At the same time Sarah Winchester was building her home in California, George Washington II was constructing his own estate in the mountains of North Carolina. But unlike Winchester, he hired the best architects and engineers of the time to design his palatial home. And he followed their plan meticulously. Today, that home is known as the Biltmore Estate. At more than 175,000 square feet, it is the largest privately-owned home in America. The Estate is still in the Vanderbilt family. It employs hundreds of people and it is the most popular tourist attraction in the State.

So, what's the difference between Winchester and Vanderbilt? One of the buildings had a plan; the other did not.

You and I will probably never build mansions like Sarah Winchester and George Washington Vanderbilt, but each of us is building something. Your financial life is like a home that you build a little bit each day – with every decision you make and every dollar you spend, adding another brick to that

Your financial life is like a home that you build a little bit each day – with every decision you make and every dollar you spend, adding another brick to that home.

home.

If you build without a plan, you will end up with your own mystery house – one filled with waste, frustration and missed opportunities. But if you get an expert plan and follow it faithfully, you will build something beautiful that will endure for generations.

God has an expert plan for your money that is designed to make your life peaceful, enjoyable and impactful. So, what exactly is God's Master Plan? It comes down to four simple things that God wants you to do with your finance. These four things can be easily noticed in the three different tithes God gave ancient Israel:

- Provide for your family
- Practice generosity
- Prepare for the future
- Enjoy and have fun

They appear simple but require a lot of work. Managing money is all about managing your priorities. Recall that I said we own nothing and God owns everything, but problems come when you decide to own and refuse to manage. God's plan works when you align your priorities with God's priorities.

> Managing money is all about managing your priorities.

This simple list reflects God's priorities regarding money and how we are to use it. Let's look at each of the four items:

1. Providing for your Family

This is pretty obvious isn't it? God wants you to ensure that those who depend on you are well cared for.

"But if anyone does not provide for his own, and especially for those of his household, he has denied the faith and is worse than an unbeliever."[1]

This may seem instinctive and simple for anyone to follow, but many stumble and struggle to do it. For some, it maybe because they are not earning enough but for the most part, many simply do not do enough to plan their needs and manage their cash flow. Most people are not intentional about how they live. They live their lives on the whims of culture and bow to the pressure of its demands. Do not let culture dictate how you live.

"Don't become so well-adjusted to your culture that you fit into it without even thinking..."[2]

Distinguishing between wants and needs would help you to better manage whatever you have. Unless you are one of those rare individuals who make more money than you have need for, you hardly ever have enough for both at the same time because no matter how much you earn, your expenses rise to meet your income all the time. It's a law - The Parkinson's law. It says that expenses rise to meet income. Actually, long before Parkinson was

> Distinguishing between wants and needs would help you to better manage whatever you have.

born, Solomon said this in his wisdom literature:

"When goods increase, they increase who eat them…"[3]

No matter how much comes into your hand, there will always be needs that rise to meet the new salary or income level you have just attained. So, guess what? You do not have a money problem. No! You just have a self-control problem. Nobody really has a money-problem; we all have a discipline problem. Here's why I know this to be true: your current habits, if not changed, will follow you to your next level of income. You will always move your current spending habits into your next financial level. Therefore, what you have always done when you have one million is what you will do when you have two million. Your habits at one million, if not changed, will remain your habits at two million, and at three million, and so on; and nothing will change that. God encourages us to plan:

"Good planning and hard work lead to prosperity, but hasty shortcuts lead to poverty."[4]

"Hasty" in this verse describes a person who jumps at a purchase without a plan and without thinking through the consequences.

The best tool for being intentional with your money is a budget. A budget is your key to living intentionally. As mentioned earlier, before

> The best tool for being intentional with your money is a budget.

you can prioritize your spending, you must differentiate between your needs and wants. After determining your needs and wants, then you can create a plan for living within your means. This is vitally important to finding success in your personal finance situation.

Everyone's life and circumstances are different but our most basic needs are universal.

"And having food and clothing, with these we shall be content."[5]

Needs are items that you **require** to survive. In actuality, they are no more than four things:

- Food, water and toiletries to maintain good health.

- Shelter – a roof over your head to protect you against the elements with the basic utilities to make the place functional. For many, this may come once a year; so, in order not to be caught off guard, set aside some money for this type of item every month.

- Clothing – just what you need to remain comfortable and appropriately dressed.

- Basic health care and hygiene.

Of course, there are other things like transportation, children's school fees, taxes, etc. These are some of the key expenses you need to plan for first before paying for anything else. If you are struggling to determine whether a certain expense is a need or want, ask yourself this clarifying question: *"If I don't buy this, will it mess up my life?"* If your answer is yes, then add it to your need list – the things you must take care of first before others.

With your needs clarified, you have a good foundation for establishing a family budget. Very few people actually do a comprehensive budget every month. Yet, a budget is the number one tool for bossing your money and aligning with God's plan for your money.

One way or another you will budget – either intentional or after the facts. Has this ever happened to you? You had a hundred thousand quid at the start of the month but in a matter of days, you had nothing left. And the sad thing is that you can't even remember what you did with it. So, in order to resolve the 'mystery', you then take a piece of paper and attempt to account for how you spent the money. Recalling and itemizing your expenses is reverse budgeting – a budget after the fact. However, if you had done that intentional at the beginning, you would have had control of the steering wheel of your finances.

> A budget is the number one tool for bossing your money and aligning with God's plan for your money.

> A budget is nothing more than a plan for giving, saving and spending money.

A budget is nothing more than a plan for giving, saving and spending money. It includes where the money will come from and how much is expected, as well as what expenses that same money will be used to meet. A good budget takes care of your key needs first and also allows for the unexpected or occasional expenses.

This is how to live within your means; it may require a paradigm shift that does away with the kind of short-sighted decision-making that says: *"If I have money right now, I can spend it right now. So, if I want new clothes today, and I have the money today, why not spend it? The rent isn't due until next week, so I'll worry about that then."*

2. Practice Generosity

I have dedicated a full chapter to this topic (see chapter 7). Practicing generosity is a struggle for many people because there are a number of misconceptions, arguments and myths. Generosity is a bit more than just giving money away, it is an expression of the radically freeing effect of true faith in Jesus Christ. It's a matter of internal liberty that results in falling in love with people and falling out of love with things.

Always remember this: All your income is not yours to consume on yourself.

> Generosity is a bit more than just giving money away, it is an expression of the radically freeing effect of true faith in Jesus Christ.

3. Prepare for the Future

"Lazy people should learn a lesson from the way ants live. They have no leader, chief or ruler, but they store up their food during the summer, getting ready for winter."[6]

In addition to providing for your family and practicing generosity, God wants you to prepare for the future.

Planning ahead and saving a part of what we earn allows us to accomplish goals, prepare for the future and be more effective in ministry. When we don't plan ahead and save money, we are more prone to go into debt, which the Bible tells us is unwise.

Jesus' story of the ten virgins reminds us of the consequences of not planning well ahead and saving for the future. The five virgins with no savings were referred to as foolish because only fools consume everything they have today without preparing for tomorrow.

Solomon says: *"...whoever gathers money little by little make it grow."[7]*

Setting aside a percentage of your income monthly will prepare you for a predictable future with little or no stress. It would help you take care of unexpected events and expenses. It will also prepare you for future projects and purchase as well as what to live on when you eventually retire and too old to work.

People who manage their resources well leave a legacy for the next generation. It will enable you empower your children – and even grandchildren – to continue making a difference with your money after you are gone.

"A good person leaves an inheritance for their children's children, but a sinner's wealth is stored up for the righteous."[8]

Of course, there are plenty of wrong motives for saving money. If we're saving money out of fear of the future, it shows we're not really trusting God to provide.

4. Enjoy and Have Fun

"Command those who are rich in this present world not to be arrogant nor to put their hope in wealth, which is so uncertain, but to put their hope in God, who rightly provides us with everything for our enjoyment."[9]

God wants you to enjoy your money. That may sound strange to a lot of people or even offend some; but the truth is right there in that scripture above. God is not a killjoy. He wants you to do whatever you do with your money for His glory and your good. So, when you are planning how to enjoy your abundance, it's important to make sure you're doing it in a life-giving, God-honouring way.

WHERE DO I BEGIN?

Once the need to budget is clearly understood, the next question may be: "Where do I start?"

Start with a vision for your financial life and write it down. What do you hope to achieve financially? Share your vision with your family and get everyone on the same page with you.

"...write what you see. Write it out in big block letters so that it can be read on the run. This vision-message is a witness pointing to what's coming..."[10]

Let the vision guide your thoughts and propel your every action. It will serve as a motivation when the going gets tough.

HOW TO BUDGET

The following are the important elements that will assist you in developing a God honouring budget for you and for your family.

1. **Budget together as a family.** If you are married, it is extremely important that you and your spouse plan the budget together. Imagine what a tremendous teaching example this can be for your children!

2. **List All of Your Expenses.** Good budgeting requires history. It would be nice to capture your current spending habits and your expenses pattern. One way

to do this is to spy on your money for about a month or two. Write down every single expense throughout the period. After about a month or two, a clear pattern will emerge because you will now know exactly how you have been spending and on what. Sometimes, a husband and wife can lead separate lives financially and have no idea what the other is doing. For a budget to work, both husband and wife must be honest about expenses. So, take a sheet of paper and list your expenses.

3. **Prioritize Your Needs.** After specifically itemizing the expenses, you need to decide which expenses are the most important and the first to be paid. Food, shelter, utilities, clothing and transportation are the basic necessities that should be at the top of the priority list as discussed earlier.

    If you do not have a steady income or if you are at a place in your life where the outgo is exceeding the income, use this process for prioritizing your needs. When one is "down in the dumps" and without a plan, it can be easy to spend recklessly.

4. **Learn to Say "No"!** No is a complete sentence. It may not be easy, but learning to say no will go a long way in helping to balance your budget and avoid the trap of debt. If it isn't in the budget, then it shouldn't be purchased at this time. Don't fall for the "buy now—pay later!" trick.

Why wait? The answer is found in the Scriptures:

"The rich rules over the poor, and the borrower is servant to the lender."[11]

The deeper in debt we get, the greater the problems for our budget and family finances.

5. Increase Your Education. Most of us would like to make more money than we currently do. Would your income improve if you were to get a degree, a trade certification or learn a new skill or trade?

   It may not be possible to go back to the university for a degree (or it may take years of night school) but there are other ways to make yourself more valuable to an employer. Take advantage of continuing-education programs that may be offered by your company or in your profession. Study and seek more advanced certifications in your field online. Perhaps, apprentice under a more knowledgeable and skilled person in your field, or seek such a person as a mentor.

   In the working world, wisdom and understanding require education. Investing wisely in your education may be one of the best financial investments that you can make.

6. Seek Wise Counsel. Turning your situation around may be a difficult process, but in addition to the wise principles of Scripture, there are numerous resources

available to you. Solomon also wrote:

"Without counsel, plans go awry, but in the multitude of counsellors they are established"[12]

Your budget is the plan; and if you need help, seek the guidance of a wise, understanding and knowledgeable counsellor.

Finally, a simple formula for your money should follow this order:

- **O** Give
- **O** Save
- **O** Spend

Note that I have not attached a percentage to these categories; but if possible, you could start with the popular 10:10:80 formula. Give a minimum of ten percent, save ten percent, and spend the balance of eighty percent.

In deciding on how best to allocate what you have in a way that honours God, let me recommend a concept in Andy Stanley's *Fields of Gold*. It is called the three 'P's of giving: Priority, Percentage and Progressiveness.

Give based on a percentage, give based on your priority, and be progressive with your giving. Besides these, be sure to offer from a grateful heart. What are you thankful for? That's where your giving should start. Apostle Paul expresses the New Testament standard for your giving so well in the following scriptures:

"So let each one give as he purposes in his heart, not grudgingly or of necessity; for God loves a cheerful giver."[13]

Chapter Five

FINANCIAL FREEDOM

———— ••●•• ————

"The real measure of your wealth is how much
you'd be worth if you lost all your money."

Anonymous

———— ••●•• ————

Financial Freedom

F inancial freedom means having enough savings, investments, and cash to afford the lifestyle you want for yourself and family and a growing nest egg that will allow you retire or pursue the career you wish to have without being driven by earning a certain amount each year. Being financially free also means that your residual or passive income equals or exceeds what you need to sustain your current lifestyle.

The Bible also preaches financial freedom but its definition is markedly different. Financial freedom, from a biblical standpoint, is freedom from the control of money and tyranny of stuff.

For us, therefore, financial freedom is not freedom from

the lack of money or having all the money you need to buy whatever you want; but being content with what you have.

How many people ever make it to that place of financial freedom as defined by culture? Again, here is an excellent question to help you determine where you are today on your journey to financial freedom. How much more money do you need to make or save to be financially free? The things we associate with having more money, or we assume a lot of money will give to us (such as love, joy, peace, freedom, etc.), are not products of physical realities but of a spiritual state. They are what the Bible calls 'Fruit of the Spirit'. For Christians, financial freedom is not a financial issue but a spiritual one. Through God's word and by His Spirit, we learn self-control.

> Financial freedom is not freedom from the lack of money, but being content with what you have.

A wonderful man named Barnabas is a model for what I am talking about here:

"...Joses, who is also called Barnabas by the apostles (which is translated Son of Encouragement), a Levite of the country of Cyprus, having land, sold it and brought the money and laid it at the apostles' feet."[1]

> For Christians, financial freedom is not a financial issue but a spiritual one.

The first thing I want to

point out here is that Barnabas was a New Testament Levite. He was one of those who should be receiving tithes under the old dispensation but he is here liquidating his asset to fund the gospel. This text was a brief introduction of this wonderful man. Later on, we will meet him as the advocate of the new convert – Paul (Acts 9:27); as shepherd of new gentile converts in Antioch (Acts 11:22); as the one trusted with relief for the poor (Acts 11:30); as the first missionary partner of Paul in his journeys (Acts 13:2); and as the advocate of giving John Mark a second chance (Acts 15:37).

He shines as one of the most trusted, mature and lovable leaders of the early church. Luke, the author of Acts of the Apostles, shows how Barnabas' trusted ministry began –with a demonstrated freedom from the love of things, and a heart of love for the poor.

Barnabas is a model of the radically freeing effect of true faith in Jesus. Following Jesus is not a matter of outward conformity to religious expectations; it is a matter of internal liberty. It's not a matter of force and law; it's a matter of freedom and love.

Being a Christian means being changed from inside out so that you fall in love with people and fall out of love with things. You cannot have both at the same time – love for people and love for things. If you love people, you will use things; but if you love

> If you love people, you will use things; but if you love things, you will use people.

things, you will use people.

Contrast the attitude of Ananias and Sapphira with that of Barnabas and you will see the hypocrisy of the heart. Nothing reveals the real state of your heart and the genuineness of your faith like your attitude towards money.

"But a certain man named Ananias, with Sapphira his wife, sold a possession. And kept back a part of the proceeds, his wife also being aware of it, and brought a certain part and laid it at the apostles' feet. But Peter said, "Ananias, why has Satan filled your heart to lie to the Holy Spirit and keep back part of the price of the land for yourself?"2

This couple loved money. They made a sale but couldn't bear giving away all the cash that came from it; so they kept some back but wanted to look more generous than they really were. They wanted the apostles to think that they were like Barnabas. They not only loved money; they also loved the praise of men (both almost always go together).

They lied to cover up their covetousness and to give an impression of being generous. If you love money and the applause of men, your love for truth will dissolve into deception and fraud. If there was any external constraint

> If you love money and the applause of men, your love for truth will dissolve into deception and fraud.

or pressure on them to give, you might want to offer them the benefit of a doubt; but this was a matter of their freewill. They were trying to fake on the outside what hasn't happened on the inside.

You see, again, nothing exposes the true condition of one's heart more than money. If you haven't experienced the transforming grace of Christ which results in genuine love for others, not only will you struggle to give, but your giving would be meaningless.

Zacchaeus was another man who experienced this transforming grace of God. He lived in Jericho. He was a chief tax collector and he was rich. Jesus entered Jericho and was passing through and Zacchaeus wanted to see who He was. But on account of the crowd, he could not – because he was of short stature. So, Zacchaeus ran on ahead and climbed up into a sycamore tree to see Jesus, for he was about to pass by that way. And when Jesus came to the place, he looked up and said to him:

> If you haven't experienced the transforming grace of Christ which results in genuine love for others, not only will you struggle to give, but your giving would be meaningless.

"Zacchaeus, hurry and come down, for I must stay at your house today."[3]

So, Zacchaeus hurried and came down. Jesus evidently confronted Zacchaeus about his sin, and he repented and believed. Now, what was the evidence of his transformation? The first and immediate evidence that Zacchaeus was a new creation in Christ was financial. As soon as he felt the waves of God's grace wash over him and renew him, Zacchaeus stood and said to Jesus:

"Behold, Lord, the half of my goods I give to the poor. And if I have defrauded anyone of anything, I restore it fourfold"[4]

Now, it is very important to notice what Jesus said to Zacchaeus. Jesus did not say, "Zacchaeus, that's great! What a wonderful gesture!" No! As soon as Zacchaeus said that he was willing to part with his money, Jesus said to him:

"Today salvation has come to this house."[5]

The evidence of Zacchaeus' transformation was his attitude toward money. As I have already mentioned, money is a spotlight on a person's spiritual condition. It is an index to a person's character and a reflection of a person's heart. It was this same transforming grace of God, which is the evidence of a genuine heart conversion that Apostle Paul referred to when he wrote to the church at Corinth about the exemplary lives of the Macedonians:

"We want you to know, brothers, about the grace of God that has been given

> Money is a spotlight on a person's spiritual condition. It is an index to a person's character and a reflection of a person's heart.

among the churches of Macedonia"[6]

The Macedonia churches consisted of three churches: in Philippi, Berea, and Thessalonica. Recall that Paul was raising money for the church in Jerusalem that was experiencing massive famine which had badly impacted the availability of food. So wherever Paul went among the Gentile churches, he asked for financial support for the church in Jerusalem.

The Macedonia churches were poor therefore Paul didn't bother to include them in the collection. He must have reasoned that they didn't have anything to give. But somehow, word got out among the Macedonians that there was this collection for the church in Jerusalem and they wanted to be a part of it. In fact, they begged (almost insisting) that they be allowed to participate:

"Entirely on their own, they urgently pleaded with us for the privilege of sharing in the service to the saints."[7]

In sharing his experience in Macedonia to help encourage the church in Corinth to rise to the occasion, here's what Paul wrote:

"Moreover, brethren, we make known to you the grace of God bestowed on the churches of Macedonia: that in a great trial of affliction, the abundance of their joy and their deep poverty abounded in the riches of their liberality. For I bear witness that according to their ability, yes, and beyond their ability, they were freely willing,

imploring us with much urgency that we would receive the gift and the fellowship of the ministering to the saints. And not only as we had hoped, but they first gave themselves to the Lord, and then to us by the will of God."[8]

The first thing to note here is that their giving was initiated by God's grace. The primary motive for their giving was not human kindness or philanthropy or the need to ease their consciences; it was not even a response to human need. No! What motivated the churches of Macedonia to give was the grace of God that had been given to them. They have been recipients of God's grace and their lives were completely transformed.

God's grace radically transforms; it completely recreates and fully re-orients anyone who comes in contact with it. Just as God's grace transformed Zacchaeus, so God's grace transformed the churches of Macedonia. And where did that grace come from? Jesus.

> God's grace radically transforms; it completely recreates and fully re-orients anyone who comes in contact with it.

"For you know the grace of our Lord Jesus Christ, that though He was rich, yet for your sakes He became poor, that you through His poverty might become rich."[9]

So, all genuine generosity is initiated by God's grace. When someone struggles to give, it's because they are yet to be truly impacted by the grace of God.

WORRY

Contentment is the cure to greed and anxiety. Just like financial freedom, worry is not a money-problem; it is a spiritual problem (and I didn't say that – Jesus did!). If money were the antidote to worry, then Jesus would have admonished that in order to get rid of worry, just get more money. Instead, He said that the reason you're worried is because you have put your trust on riches rather than on He who richly provides. That's the sole reason people worry.

"Therefore, I tell you, do not worry about your life, what you will eat or drink; or about your body, what you will wear. Is not life more than food, and the body more than clothes? Look at the birds of the air; they do not sow or reap or store away in barns, and yet your heavenly Father feeds them. Are you not much more valuable than they? Can any of you by worrying add a single hour to your life? "And why do you worry about clothes? See how the flowers of the field grow. They do not labour or spin. Yet I tell you that not even Solomon in all his splendour was dressed like one of these. If that is how God clothes the grass of the field which is here today and tomorrow is thrown into the fire, will he not much more clothe you, o you of little faith!? So do not worry, saying, 'What shall we eat?' or 'What shall we drink?' or 'What shall we wear?' For the pagans run after all these things, and your heavenly Father knows

that you need them. But seek first his kingdom and his righteousness, and all these things will be given to you as well. Therefore, do not worry about tomorrow, for tomorrow will worry about itself. Each day has enough trouble of its own."[10]

The antidote for worry is faith in God; not hope that God will give us money, but trust that God's grace will be available to us regardless of our financial circumstances. The problem of the average person (or should I say Nigerian) is that we think all problems can be solved by prayer. If you have been taught for a long time that prayer is the 'master key', it is hard not to hold such a view. But the truth is there is no master key anywhere. Jesus said:

"And I will give you the keys of the kingdom of heaven..."[11]

Take note that the *keys* are plural.

Prayer in the life of a Christian is critical, and God is interested in our needs and desires. Praying to God is an indicator that we are humble and dependent on Him for our everyday life; but prayer is not a substitute for seeking knowledge and wisdom. Financial intelligence and acumen are necessary for anyone who wants to be

Praying to God is an indicator that we are humble and dependent on Him for our everyday life; but prayer is not a substitute for seeking knowledge and wisdom.

financially successful. There is a know-how that is acquired for making and keeping the money you make.

It is often said that money talks, but if you do not understand the language of money, the only thing your money will be saying is 'bye' which sounds very much like 'buy'. God didn't create money, and that's why there are no Pound Sterling or Dollars or Yen in the Bible; instead, God created resources. Money is an invention of man. Therefore, man must learn the mechanics and dynamics of how money works in order to gain mastery over it.

Money and financial success are not the exclusive preserve of Christians; the only difference is that as a Christian, you have God's guide in His word on how to relate with it. The point I am making is that you should learn how money works. Buy books, attend seminars, find a mentor and learn as much as you can. God may give you insights and ideas that could lead to substantial financial harvests, but without proper knowledge on how to retain and grow the income from such a sense, you are soon back to square one.

Chapter Six

MONEY: SECURITY RISK

—••●●••—

"I would like to live as a poor man
with a lot of money."

Pablo Picasso (1881 – 1973)
Spanish Artist and Poet

—••●••—

Money: Security Risk

•••••

It is often said that money 'talks'. What it means is that money gives you leverage. It is common knowledge that money gives you a voice – we listen to affluent people. There is a subtle arrogance that comes with having money because it gives you an inflated sense of importance. It could lead you to think that what you have to say is more important than what anyone else has to say. There is even a belief I think has gained acceptance in our culture, that if someone is financially successful, then that person is better than others of lesser means. Nothing could be more flawed. That is why Apostle Paul instructed Timothy to:

"Command those who are rich in this present age not to be

haughty, nor to trust in uncertain riches but in the living God, who gives us richly all things to enjoy."[1]

God understands this dark side of money. Without even realizing it, the more money you have, the easier it is for your identity to be shaped by what you have rather than by who you are in Christ (and the culture we live in makes that so much easier). We live in a culture where money often defines who we are; therefore, our identity can quickly be wrapped around the size of our house, the coolness of our car, our job title or the side of town we live in.

Clive Hamilton and Richard Denniss, authors of the book *Affluenza*, say:

"It is not money and material possessions that are the root of the problem; it is our attachment to them and the way they condition our thinking, give us our self-definition and rule our lives."

Sadly, in our culture today, our bank balance and the toys we can collect now serve as a ready indicator of our achievement and how much we are worth, personally. However, it would have been all right if it all ends there, but it Our ability to stack up money and assets is too shallow to be the base for life satisfaction. Money not only has the capacity to distort the view of our identity, the identity it offers is very fragile – one that can easily be crushed by changing circumstances.

never does. We wrongly try to make it a base for satisfaction in life. Our ability to stack up money and assets is too shallow to be the base for life satisfaction. Money not only has the capacity to distort the view of our identity, the identity it offers is very fragile – one that can easily be crushed by changing circumstances.

As I have mentioned already, one reason Jesus talks so much about money in the Gospels is that He knows the dark side of money; He knows that the primary competitor with God for the throne of your heart is not the devil, but money and the things money can buy. Jesus knows the seductive power of money. He knows how it can subtly displace God in your heart without you even realizing it.

When your identity gets wrapped up in what you have rather than who you are, it becomes more difficult to be generous. You will have a tendency to cling to whatever you have as if your life depends on it. Why? Because giving away even a tiny piece of your possessions will feel like giving away a part of your identity – and that can be scary!

> When your identity gets wrapped up in what you have rather than who you are, it becomes more difficult to be generous.

As Christians, we should base our identity not on what we have, but on Christ and what He generously did for us on the cross of Calvary.

There is a danger even more significant than finding

your identity in what you possess – that of finding security in what you have, rather than in God. The parable of the rich fool, which we looked at earlier, depicts the falseness of the belief that wealth can secure the future. Greed promises security, but cannot deliver it. It is a deceitful desire.

Money cannot give protection; that's why the Bible says not to trust it. The irony is that the more money you have, the more vulnerable and less secure you feel. Why? Because now you have a lot more at stake. It is the fear of losing what you have (or not having enough) that fuels insecurity and feeds the greed-nature. Wealth offers a false sense of security. Solomon says:

"The wealth of a rich man is their fortified city; they imagine it a wall too high to scale."[2]

The Bible tells a story about a rich young ruler who came to Jesus. He was a typical urban professional – doing very well financially, young, upward, mobile, hard-working, decent, sincere, and desperately wanting peace in his life. He wanted to know what he must do to inherit eternal life but he was blinded by the security of his great possessions.

"...Good Teacher, what shall I do that I may inherit eternal life?... You know the commandments: 'Do not

commit adultery; 'Do not murder; 'Do not steal; 'Do not bear false witness; 'Do not defraud; 'Honor your father and your mother'." And he answered and said to Him, "Teacher, all these things I have kept from my youth" Then Jesus, looking at him, loved him, and said to him, "One thing you lack: Go your way, sell whatever you have and give to the poor, and you will have treasure in heaven; and come, take up the cross, and follow Me." But he was sad at this word, and went away sorrowful, for he had great possessions."3

This young man wants to go to heaven. He lived an upright and moral life, he had a desire to follow Christ, and no doubt he thought he was ready from any standpoint. It never crossed his mind that his money (or how he viewed it) was a hindrance to him. He thought keeping the commands of God was more than enough but didn't realize his money had blinded him. This is the dark side of money; if you let it compete with Jesus for the throne of your heart, it has a good chance of winning.

Jesus said "…*go sell what you have*"! Why? He knew this man had the wrong attitude towards money that needed to change for him to get his desire; but the young man turned and walked away. He was young and upright, kept the law, loved by Jesus but ruled by money. This could be you, yet you are not even aware! His desire to go to heaven was all about him, not God or anyone else.

Does wealth and riches define you? Has it become your silent or salient source of security? What of the subtle arrogance that comes with being able to do whatever you like because you have the means? Rather than call on God, you call on the almighty Dollar.

> *Money is good for what it is good for, but for all its worth, if you are not enough without it, you will never be enough with it.*

Your heavenly Father clearly is not against you becoming wealthy or prosperous – provided your priorities are not misplaced. Money is good for what it is good for, but for all its worth, if you are not enough without it, you will never be enough with it.

There are, at least, four solid guardrails on money that the Bible sets up for us:

1. **Don't waste it.** Your money is not yours; you are merely a manager. God will, someday, call your stewardship of His resources to account. You don't want to waste God's money.

2. **Don't love it.** It's impossible to live with a divided allegiance. You cannot have two number ones in your life. You cannot have a love for money and God as your number one goal. Decide: Is God or money your number one goal in life? You cannot serve them both.

3. **Don't trust it.** No matter how much you have; you can

lose it.

"In the blink of an eye, money can disappear, as if it grew wings and flew away like a bird."[4]

4. **Don't expect it to satisfy.** Howard Hughes, a famed billionaire, was asked, "How much more does it take to make a man happy?" He replied, "Just a little bit more." The Bible says,

"Whoever loves money never has enough; whoever loves wealth is never satisfied with their income."[5]

Chapter Seven

GENEROSITY

"We make a living by what we get, but we make a life by what we give.

Winston Churchill
(Former British Prime Minister)

Generosity

Often, when we think about generosity or a generous person, we think of a rich person who always gives away large sums of money from time to time. Yet, if you ask many whether they are generous, most (if not all) will say yes.

So, what is generosity? The dictionary defines generosity as the quality of being kind, understanding and not selfish; the quality of being generous, especially willing to give money and other valuable things to others.

J.I Parkard, in his book, *Knowing God*, provides us with a definition of generosity I like. He says generosity means: The disposition to give to others in a way that has no selfish motive and is not limited by what the recipient deserves, but continually goes beyond it.

Generosity is more than a random or spontaneous act of giving things away. In the impulsive act of giving to someone (or a group of people), a demand or request must be made by someone for a need to be met. Usually, they advertise the need or bring to the knowledge of a target audience. Then everybody is asked to contribute so they could meet the demand. Depending on the persuasive skill of the person doing the pitch, many will give; but the majority of those who give will give out of guilt, pity, or obligation. Rarely is such giving done without some kind of pressure. This kind of giving is not pre-planned or predetermined but is sporadic and spontaneous. This does not imply that giving in this way is wrong, but it's not the best way to give, and it doesn't fit our definition of generosity.

Churches do this often (it even assumes a dimension sometimes). The common practice is for the preacher or his representative to present a need. Then he calls out for people who would like to give a certain amount of money over the specified timeline to step forward. In most cases, he will name a particular figure or a bracket (say, 10-20 million) and ask those who would give an amount in that bracket to come forward. Depending on the congregation, some people may respond immediately. If the pledges from the first set of respondents fall short of the target amount, the call continues (but with a lower bracket - to accommodate more people). This cycle may continue till the lowest bracket is eventually called or until they reach the desired target.

If you are in the audience when this kind of fundraising takes place (and depending on your standing or perceived status in the gathering), you will feel the emotional pressure to respond. More often than not, you will feel forced to decide when you have not really thought your actions through. Therefore, many people who make commitments under such circumstances eventually struggle to redeem their obligations.

Depending on how often this happens, some people will become known for their regular donations and contributions; hence, they become classified within that community as being generous. But, on the contrary, that isn't generosity! That is spontaneous or random giving! Generosity is different; it is a cultivated habit or a way of living that isn't altogether instinctive.

While generosity is no longer natural to man because of sin, some societies have deliberately inculcated generosity into the fabric of their culture. For instance, the Western worlds, because of their deep Christian roots, have a culture of kindness. In these societies, people are generous or expected to be generous. Conversely, in Africa, not only do we not have a natural inclination to give,

> Generosity is different; it is a cultivated habit or a way of living that isn't altogether instinctive.

we do not have the culture of being generous. Africans do not have a giving culture. In fact, depending on where you are from, your generosity could be viewed with suspicion. Unsolicited kindness from a stranger could be considered as having an ulterior motive or diabolical intent. To become a generous person (which is who God wants you to be), you need to overcome a few myths about who is, or who can be generous. There are at least five basic myths about generosity:

1. **Generous People Are Rich People.** No! Generous people are generous; rich people are rich. Being generous is a habit of the heart and a mentality. There is no correlation between riches and generosity. There is no correlation between a person's bank account and his generosity. Instead, research has shown that the more people have, the less they give. In the story about a widow who gave two mites in the synagogue, Jesus' remarks about who gave the most must have shocked His disciples when He said,

   "This widow gave the most because she gave her all. Others gave from their abundance."[6]

   Research, all over the world, has shown that rich folks are not the most generous. Wealthier people give less when compared to their percentage income.

2. **Generosity Depends on Cash Flow.** People say this all the time: *"You know the reason I don't give; it is because I don't have enough. When I have, or when*

more resources come into my hands, or when I earn my salary, then I will be generous." No, you won't! The truth of the matter is that generosity has nothing to do with cash flow; it is not determined by or dependent on cash flow. Generosity, like faithfulness, is a character trait; it doesn't come circumstantially. If you're not generous today and you do not learn how to be generous, you won't be generous tomorrow – no matter how much you have.

3. **Generosity is Difficult.** When you imagine situations where you are goaded into donating more money than you can afford or being forced to give up a prized possession to benefit someone else, you are likely to believe this myth. However, try looking at generosity as something you get to do, instead of something you should do. Practising generosity can make you realize that some of the best ways to give are also fun and enjoyable!

> Practising generosity can make you realize that some of the best ways to give are also fun and enjoyable!

4. **Generosity is Spontaneous.** The truth is: Generous people are not necessarily impulsive people, neither are they necessarily emotional with their giving. They are, more often than not, strategic with their giving.

5. **It is the Amount that Counts.** Many people assume that when someone can give a large sum of money, it means that the person is generous. Nothing can be

farther from the truth. We compare donations made by individuals and determine who is more generous based on the amount given. Jesus turned this myth on its head in the widow's story. Part of the lesson from that story is that sometimes, the sacrifice speaks louder than the size of the gift:

"Jesus sat down opposite the place where the offerings were put and watched the crowd putting their money into the temple treasury. Many rich people threw in large amounts. But a poor widow came and put in two very small copper coins, worth only a few cents. Calling his disciples to him, Jesus said, "Truly I tell you; this poor widow has put more into the treasury than all the others. They all gave out of their wealth; but she, out of her poverty, put in everything—all she had to live on."[7]

A gentle challenge for all of us would be to consider increase our giving (whether money, time, or talents) beyond convenience into the realm of sacrifice.

Generous people are not necessarily impulsive people, neither are they necessarily emotional with their giving. They are, more often than not, strategic with their giving.

CHARACTERISTICS OF GENEROUS PEOPLE

1. Generous People Often Give More than the Minimum

The children of Israel wanted to build a Tabernacle:

"Then Moses called Bezalel and Aholiab, and every gifted artisan in whose heart the Lord had put wisdom, everyone whose heart was stirred, to come and do the work. And they received from Moses all the offering which the children of Israel had brought for the work of the service of making the sanctuary. So, they continued bringing to him freewill offerings every morning. ...So, Moses gave a commandment and they caused it to be proclaimed throughout the camp, saying "Let neither man nor woman do any more work for the offering of the sanctuary." And the people were restrained from bringing, for the material they had was sufficient for all the work to be done – indeed too much."[8]

We see God's people bringing more than enough to meet the need (to the point that Moses must tell them to stop!). Today, it is rare to see where givers are asked to stop giving! But when it does happen, it's a special moment. Giving to a cause that makes you reach for your very best gift can bring some of the greatest fulfilment you'll ever know! Truly generous people are often not satisfied with doing just the minimum

2. Generous People Give In Response to a Great Cause

The churches in Macedonia and Corinth gave faithfully to help a community of people in Judea whom they have never met! It doesn't matter who gets the benefit; as long as it's a good cause, generous people don't hold back.

3. Generous People Give More than Just Their Money

In Luke 10:25-37, Jesus tells the classic story of the Good Samaritan – one who gave time, resources, and skill to meet the need of a man who had been left for dead at the side of the road. The Samaritan makes himself vulnerable and available (the exact definition of hospitality). Generosity and hospitality are often closely linked.

In today's culture, more generous givers want to give more than just their financial resources. This is especially true of younger givers; they want to get their feet on the ground with the causes they're supporting. Volunteering with an organization you're passionate about is a great way to find a deeper connection to the cause. And sometimes (as in the story of the Good Samaritan), the opportunity is right there in front of you– without you having to search for it.

Jump in with whatever you should give – money, time, skills, etc. – and see what God will do both in you and through you.

4. Generous People Give Even When it Doesn't Make Sense

In Genesis 45, we find Joseph responding graciously and generously to his family even when logic would tell him not to. Sometimes, giving to a project or cause makes no sense to anyone but you! Like Joseph, you may have been mistreated or harmed in some way (by a church or a cause); yet, you still believe in the mission of the organization even though there are hard feelings.

This kind of situation gets at the very heart of your commitment to being a generous person.

Moving beyond our humanity is the hardest thing to overcome. Setting aside differences in order to help do the right thing with your generosity is an act of real maturity – true Christ-likeness.

5. Generous People Give To Help Others, Even When They Differ From One Another

In Luke 7:1-10, we see a Gentile who built a Jewish synagogue! Who could have predicted such a donor for such a cause? Sometimes, we're given opportunities to help people outside of our worldview.

Of course, your conscience has to guide you as to how and where to invest your resources; it is healthy to keep an open mind, to genuinely consider the potential of various projects to accomplish something good and valuable, and to imagine yourself contributing to such an endeavour. It may become a character-growth opportunity for you and a boon to that worthwhile project.

6. Generous People Demonstrate Personal Transformation.

The story of Zacchaeus (Luke 19) is the story of a transformed giver. What a beautiful story – a tax collector forsaking the norm in order to give (moved by Jesus' call to come back to God's ways)!

This is the story of someone who morphs from "collector of money" to "giver of money"! Perhaps, the most deeply satisfying stories are those of people who have been radically transformed in their giving due to a spiritual transformation.

This, in a way, is a picture of redemption–as people rise above their personal limitations and see the supernatural potential of their own lives through their generous giving.

7. Poverty is not a Barrier to a Generous Person

"We want you to know, brothers, about the grace of God that has been given among the churches of Macedonia, for in a severe test of affliction, their abundance of joy and their extreme poverty have overflowed in a wealth of generosity on their part. For they gave according to their

means, as I can testify, and beyond their means, of their own accord, begging us earnestly for the favour of taking part in the relief of the saints – and this, not as we expected, but they gave themselves first to the Lord and then by the will of God to us."9

God's love always compels the generous to help those in need, even when they are in need themselves. Despite their difficult circumstances, they continue to seek God's heart of love for others.

8. Generous People Give Even When Others Will Not

In Philippians 4:15-16, the apostle Paul laments the lack of response from the churches he's encountered.

"Not one church shared with me," he says. "Only you, the Christians at Philippi.

Even when he was ministering to others far away in Thessalonica, the Philippians were giving to his ministry.

Most givers I've known like to be part of a larger giving community. It is satisfying, perhaps comforting or reassuring, to know that you're one of many giving toward a project. Yet sometimes, we are called upon as givers to stand alone, to see a project through to completion even when others won't. This is the kind of situation in which Paul found himself. Others ignored the need, but one church –at Philippi – was willing to give, to provide the needed support (even if it meant standing alone).

The day may come when you find yourself here too: You look around, and no one else is giving; but something inside you says, *"Go for it."* Your personal impact can be enormous and your personal journey can be beautifully enriched for the experience.

Generosity is not something that comes later after you accumulate wealth. It is something you live out wherever you are in life today. It is not something that "shows up"; it is a lifestyle you cultivate.

> The more generous you are and the more ways you are generous, the richer you become!

Generous people in our culture are no different from the generous people mentioned in the Bible. Generosity becomes part of a person's DNA; it permeates every area of their lives.

How generous are **you**? And just as important a question: How are you generous? These are questions worth examining. The more generous you are and the more ways you are generous, the richer you become!

> Generous people always have a giving plan. They are proactive with their giving.

One of the key differences between being generous and being merely spontaneous is that an impulsive giver needs to be made aware of or stumbles upon a need. In which case, if there weren't a request, he or she would not have given anything because there was no previous plan to do so. While a generous person doesn't have to know of a need to be liberal or to give. Generous people always have a giving plan. They are proactive with their giving.

DEVELOP A GIVING PLAN

You can learn to become a generous person and one of the few things you can start doing right away is to develop a giving plan. This will ensure that your giving is not driven by circumstances. However, it doesn't mean that you will not give randomly sometimes; but on the whole, more often structured than random. Pre-plan your giving by deciding on what percentage of your income you will give regularly (say, monthly). If you adopt percentage giving, you will give more because your giving will increase with your income. Your giving will no longer be circumstantial and you will be free of any emotional blackmail in a high-pressure fund-raising environment.

I have been in these kinds of situations many times and I am certain you have, too (especially if you have been a Christian for a while). I remember a particular incidence when a visiting preacher decided to 'raise' an offering in a church I was attending at that time. As a leader in that local assembly, I had some bit of inside knowledge, so I knew that the Senior Pastor didn't request the guest minister to call for an offering. I guess he thought it was the thing to do or maybe it was a favour to his host. What was apparent was that the man had a few people in mind he expected would heed his call, and I was one of them. When that didn't happen, he couldn't hide his disappointment after a protracted call; he then began to berate a section of the congregation –which included yours truly. His host was visibly embarrassed and had to send him a note. The man obviously wanted to force our hand by shaming or *"guilting"* us to give, but the host pastor knew how generous many of those in the congregation were.

> In your giving plan, you can pre-decide what you will give to, whom you will give to, or where you will give it.

In your giving plan, you can pre-decide what you will give to, whom you will give to, or where you will give it. This will ensure that you get the highest value and fulfilment from your giving because you can give to what is dearest to your heart. This will make you a cheerful giver and a happier person – which is what the Lord loves (2 Corinthians 9:7). A giving plan will ensure that you consume less (which is a good cure for materialism), sets your money free and sets you free from your money.

> Humility is an integral part of a generosity spirit.

NEVER BLOW YOUR OWN TRUMPET

Learn to be discreet. Motive is everything. A generous person never wants to advertise his generosity. The whole idea of calling people out not only pile pressure on people but create an unnecessary advertisement. Jesus counselled us not to let our right hand know what our left hand is doing when it comes to our generosity, but I have been in meetings where church leaders explained that away: *"...Giving to God is not the same as alms."*

Showing-off is a big deal in our culture, and we have allowed that to slip through our doors. Question any man's generosity when he sets out to make noise about it. Those who are genuinely generous are self-effacing; they have no arrogance about them. Humility is an integral part of a generosity spirit. The recipient of their generosity affirms them by telling others and instigating praise to God. We admire kindness when we see it and that's why we are moved to tell others about it. Why even try to blow your own horn when others will do it for you even if you didn't ask for it?

GENEROSITY BEGINS WITH EYES

Generous people have eyes for needs. They can spot a need from a mile, and when they see one, they never rest until something is done about it. In Matthew 25, Jesus talks about separating the sheep from the goats on Judgment day in a symbolic reference to those who are His true followers and those who are not. The key difference would be in how generous we have been to those in need:

*"...for I was hungry, and you gave Me food; I was thirsty, and you gave Me to drink.....Then the righteous will answer Him saying, 'Lord, when did we **see** You hungry and feed You, or thirsty and gave you to drink?"*[10] (emphasis mine).

It's often said that, "Eyes that look, are common; but eyes that see, are few." How sensitive are you to the needs of others? Through a life open to the community, we learn the needs of others. Admittedly, in a broken world, we all have problems, needs and desires; but we can't afford to be caught navel-gazing. Becoming generous doesn't exempt us from those. So, raise your head, look ahead and look around.

MAKE ROOM

Once you start needing boxes and more storage spaces, it is a signal you have too much. Whether its shoes, clothes, or garages, the other word for the surplus is junk and they are standing in the way of new

> Developing a generous heart is having little or no emotional or sentimental attachment to things.

ones. Developing a generous heart is having little or no emotional or sentimental attachment to things. The truth is that you will have to give them up sooner or later – voluntarily or not! So, why not give them up on purpose and experience the joy of transforming lives. If you are holding on to something you haven't used in the last three months, it's time to clear out and make more room.

"One person gives freely, yet gains even more; another withholds unduly, but comes to poverty."[11]

JUST SAY YES

God wants to use you; and no, you do not have to hear a strange and fearful voice calling out to you. He is using loads of people, and it all begins with a simple yes. A little boy offered Jesus his meagre lunch in Matthew 14:14 - 21 he only had a few loaves and fishes, and Jesus had 5,000 mouths to feed. But gifts in God's hands can be – and often are – divinely multiplied to meet the demands of greater works. This is one of the greatest giving stories; a beautiful picture of the faith to see something profound happen because you said yes.

First and foremost, the young man had enough faith to give his own lunch away! He was risking his own provision and comfort in the hope of helping others. One boy's faith is what set in motion the amazing miracle of Jesus feeding the 5,000 men (add women and children and we could be talking about 12,000 people)! Sometimes, we have to be willing to imagine something much greater than ourselves in order to get behind a project.

> Sometimes, we have to be willing to imagine something much greater than ourselves in order to get behind a project.

Don't make the mistake most people make to think generosity is primarily a financial decision. It is not! Your relationship with money is never a financial one; it is as spiritual as spiritual gets. It is the barometer for measuring your maturity and spirituality. Jesus said:

"Do not lay up for yourselves treasure on the earth where moth and rust destroy or where thieves break in and steal. But lay up for yourselves treasures in heaven where neither moth nor rust destroys and where thieves do not break in and steal."[12]

Jesus is affirming that it is good to lay treasures; but the question is, where? "For where your treasure is, there your heart will be also." God is not after your treasure; He is after your heart. He knows how your heart travels. When He gets hold of your treasure, He knows your heart will follow it.

For instance, if you invest all of your money in the shares of a particular company on the stock exchange, without a doubt, you will become immediately interested in how the company is performing. Before your investment, you probably had no care for the company and its performance; but as soon as you put your money in it, you are drawn to every detail; you will monitor the movements of its share price.

Our Lord Jesus is saying, more or less, that every one of us worships something or someone. Where your money goes tells you what or who you worship; and whatever or whoever that is, is who you look to for security, significance, and happiness. For some, it could be success in life or business; for others, it could be a career, kids, appearance or Jesus.

The bottom line is this: whatever or whoever that is, will eventually demand your life. It might even require you to die just to get him/her (or it). Therefore, if you want to know who or what you worship, check your cheque stubs or bank statement – your heart goes where your money flows. **The mirror of your soul is your money.** Joe Biden, former US Vice President, says, *"Don't tell me what you value, show me your budget, and I will tell you what you value."*

Chapter Eight

THE GENIUS OF GENEROSITY

————•◦●◦•————

"Not everything that can be counted counts,
and not everything that counts can be counted."

Albert Einstein (1879 – 1955)
Theoretical Physicist

••◦●◦••

The Genius Of Generosity

W e often think of generosity as a personality trait (i.e. you're generous or you're not). Generosity is a practice. Real generosity is a habit. It is something you can cultivate in your life. Even better, practising generosity offers a wealth of opportunities for learning about yourself, the surrounding people, and the world. Beyond spiritual demands and benefits, generosity can have a significant impact on our quality of life.

Practising generosity offers a wealth of opportunities for learning about yourself, the surrounding people, and the world.

While most people's first association with charity is making monetary donations, it is pertinent to mention that generosity is not limited to giving money. It's easy to think you can't be generous without having extra cash on hand, but free acts of kindness can sometimes be even more meaningful and valuable to an individual or organization in need. If you have the character of a generous person, you will give everything – money, time, and talent, even your life. One of the best lessons you can learn from being generous is that its effects reach farther than you could ever intend. In most cases, the payoffs for giving are instantaneous. Some immediate benefits include:

> It's easy to think you can't be generous without having extra cash on hand, but free acts of kindness can sometimes be even more meaningful and valuable to an individual or organization in need.

1. Emotional Payoffs

"In everything I did, I showed you that by this kind of hard work we must help the weak, remembering the words the Lord Jesus himself said: 'It is more blessed to give than to receive.'"[1]

Apostle Paul recalls a promise made by Jesus, that a generous person would live a happier life. Lately, science has been catching up with this promise. There is an entire body of research that explores the relationship between generosity and happiness. Many studies link the two, showing that giving can increase self-esteem, increase one's sense of purpose and decrease symptoms of depression.

Physically, generosity can lead to a decrease in stress, chronic pain intensity and mortality; while promoting higher levels of functioning. Most people feel good when they give to others – whether it's a family gift-exchange or a donation to a charity (you're probably familiar with the feeling). But only in recent years was the relationship between giving and happiness confirmed by research.

Harvard Business School researchers, in 2009, published a paper that discusses past evidence for this relationship alongside original research of their own. The paper examines whether giving promotes happiness or vice versa; and how charities use this to market their causes. They concluded that charitable giving and happiness may have a cyclical effect, and the best way to advertise charities is to appeal to that joy of giving (the amount given may not matter at all).

> Giving can increase self-esteem, increase one's sense of purpose and decrease symptoms of depression.

The same Harvard researchers conducted an original experiment in which they gave shoppers money to either spend on themselves or on someone else. The amount given to shoppers varied between $5 and $20, but when they conducted a survey later that day, the dollar amounts were inconsequential. Those who had spent the money on others rated their moods better than those who had spent it on themselves.

You may think happiness is highly individual and therefore difficult to generalize, but studies provide evidence to the contrary. Research shows that once we meet our basic needs, income level does little to affect overall happiness. Instead, satisfaction may be influenced more strongly by the perception of wealth relative to others. In giving it away, the opposite appears to hold true – those who give a higher percentage of their assets away are happier, overall.

> Research shows that once we meet our basic needs, income level does little to affect overall happiness.

Other studies suggest that when a giver sees a clear link between their actions and a positive outcome for someone in need, they may release positive hormones like oxytocin, serotonin, endorphins, and dopamine. Generosity can even extend life expectancy. When you can give of yourself selflessly, the potential windfall can be significant and it all comes relatively quickly.

The act of giving can also serve as a reminder to be thankful for what you have. Gratitude is a critical concept in happiness research. Recognizing opportunities to be grateful for things, experiences, and people can make a big difference in your emotional state.

There are two kinds of giving: transactional giving and transformational giving. If we give solely so we can get something in return (whether recognition, approval or even more money), that's transactional giving. Transactional giving ultimately can make us unhappy because it disconnects us from our own heart's desires to do good and also disconnects us from the people or cause we are giving to. Selfish individuals give only where the compensation is equal or greater in proportion to the contribution. This way of giving sinks to the level of a business deal designed to promote selfish social gains and self-glorification. Pure deeds of the Spirit are performed with no thought or hope of gain or reward and cannot be compensated for in real terms.

> Selfish individuals give only where the compensation is equal or greater in proportion to the contribution.

True generosity, as with love, is a quality of the soul that expresses kindness, beneficence, mercy, and tolerance. If our primary motive in giving is to connect with others to create change, that's transformational generosity. What we get back (a sense of happiness and purpose) is not the reason we give, but it's a beautiful side effect that spurs us on to do even more. God loves trans-formational givers; the Bible says so:

"God loves a cheerful giver."[2]

It is also the reason obligatory giving is unpleasant. Obligatory giving hardly makes anyone happy; instead, it produces resentment because it is usually done out of duty rather than devotion. Although we never should give with the intention to gain something in return from the Lord, He blesses a faithful giver. I have found that generous people tend to be healthier financially but I think the reason is not necessarily because more money came to them as a result of their generosity but because the power of greed and the addiction to things have been broken over their lives and as a result they tend to handle money in a much healthier way.

> Obligatory giving hardly makes anyone happy; instead, it produces resentment because it is usually done out of duty rather than devotion.

We should give only as an act of love and worship. The study notes for 2 Corinthians 9:11 (Fire Bible: Global Edition) puts it this way:

"For us to express true generosity outwardly, our hearts must become rich in true love and compassion for others. We should always pray and ask God to give us this kind of heart for others. Giving of ourselves and our possessions results in supplying the needs of those who are lacking in some way, praise and thanksgiving to God, and love from those who receive our help."

2. Community-Building

Nothing brings people together, like generosity. It is the simplest way to bond with people who care about the same things you do even if you start out as a stranger. Research has shown that giving improves cooperation and helps people view each other more positively. Generosity also has a vast potential for deepening close friendships. It is hard to beat relationships built on a foundation of mutual charity and the trust that comes from knowing the other person has your back. This was the experience of the first-century church in Jerusalem. The disciples of Jesus learned that five loaves and two fishes could feed five thousand people if surrendered for the good of all. So, when Jesus left, they sold houses and lands.

"They sold property and possessions to give to anyone who had need. Every day they continued to meet together in the temple courts. They broke bread in their homes and ate together with glad and sincere hearts, praising God and enjoying the favour of all the people. And the Lord added to their number daily those who were being saved."[3]

It is hard to beat relationships built on a foundation of mutual charity and the trust that comes from knowing the other person has your back.

Apostle Paul tells the Corinthians what to expect as reward for their acts of generosity:

"Now he who supplies seed

to the sower and bread for food will also supply and increase your store of seed and will enlarge the harvest of your righteousness."4

So in the real sense, our harvest from the sowing of financial seed is not more money but the harvest of righteousness. When we hear the word righteousness we tend to think only of moral and upright behaviour but it's more than that. Righteousness is right relationships – rightly relating to God and man.

Therefore the harvest of our generosity is so much more exciting than what a few extra bucks can give. What we reap as the harvest of our generosity is the healing and the restoring of the world. We get to be at the centre of God's restoring and redeeming mission in the earth. We get to be change agents and prime movers of God's agenda towards the eradication of abject poverty, of the excluded and marginalized being brought in; of the healing and reconciliation of families and communities to one another and to Him. Who would argue that isn't so much rewarding than the momentary thrill of a few extra cash?

A single act of generosity on your part can have a significant impact on more people than just your intended recipient.

Generosity, in the first-century church, created an irresistible community that magnetized un-believers. A Harvard study found that a single person acting in generosity influences observers to behave generously later. Those who observe the observers are also more likely to be generous. A single act of generosity on your part can have a significant impact on more people than just your intended recipient. The ripple effects can reach dozens or even hundreds of people; many of whom you may never know about. Making the conscious decision to practice generosity every day can feel daunting at first; but once you begin, the benefits of your choices can make it difficult to stop.

3. Good Health

The adverse health effects of depression and sadness are apparent, but what about the benefits of feeling good? The connection between happiness and giving might be obvious, but more recent research sheds light on the health benefits of happiness.

Research reveals that happiness, especially in older people, is good for the heart. In a thorough study of over 200 adults followed over 3 years, London researchers found that the happier subjects had lower blood pressure. In the same survey, happier men had lower resting heart rates, which is an indicator of heart health. They also found that those who rated their happiness higher had lower levels of the stress hormone, cortisol; and that their bodies regulated cortisol more effectively. They have implicated cortisol as a factor in many health disorders, including Type 2 diabetes and inflammatory conditions.

Harvard researchers also conducted a study that showed how giving is such a powerful immune booster and how it can be experienced just by watching someone else give! In this famous experiment, students attending a film of Mother Teresa as she tended the sick in Calcutta, got an increase in immune function (including those who purported to dislike Mother Teresa!).

Chapter Nine

THE SECRET OF CONTENTMENT

"To be content with little is difficult; to be content with much, impossible,"

Marie von Ebner-Eschenbach (1830 – 1916)
Austrian Writer

The Secret Of Contentment

 know what it is to be in need, and I know what it is to have plenty. I have learned the secret of being content in any and every situation, whether well-fed or hungry, whether living in plenty or want."[1]

Apostle Paul makes such a huge statement quoted as a rider to the Chapter. The letters from Paul to churches and individuals across the non-Jewish nations make up more than a third of the New Testament. The above quoted Scripture was a letter to the church in Philippi in modern day Turkey.

I know I have touched a bit on contentment in the previous chapters, but I still feel the need to linger a little longer on the subject because it is such a big deal in our culture today. The advent of social media has escalated the levels of discontent in the lives of many, including Christians. Apostle Paul reminds Timothy, his protégé, that

"Godliness and contentment is great gain"[2]

and shares why discontent can be very harmful to our faith. Our society today is marked by 'inextinguishable discontent'. Our quest is for a better, bigger, newer, shinier, faster, easier and all the '...ers' of this world.

Rick Ezell, Pastor and Author, whom I have quoted extensively here, writes:

"We want a better job with better pay and a better boss. We want better relationships and a better car and a better backhand in tennis or a longer drive in golf. And we have a propensity to live endlessly for the next thing – the next weekend, the next vacation, the next purchase, and the next experience. We are never satisfied, never content, and envious of those who have what we have not attained or accumulated."

Our high mobility these days reflects the extent of our discontent. People rarely stay at the same address for over five years. We are always on the move – looking for a better house, a better job, a better place to live and raise a family, a better place to retire, even a better marriage. It is part of the reason for the high divorce rate; we can't find happiness in our marriages, so we trade in our mates for new ones, only to realize that we are still discontented.

The word 'content' comes from a Greek word that means self-sufficient or independent. The Stoics elevated the word to the ability to be free from all wants and needs, as the chief of all virtues. But detachment marked Stoic philosophy from one's emotions and indifference to the vagaries of life. This is not the sense in which Paul implied the word because he communicated his feelings. Paul's view was not the pagan view of self-sufficiency, but an affirmation of the sufficiency of Christ.

Contentment isn't denying one's feelings about wanting and desiring what they can't have; instead, it exhibits freedom from being controlled by those feelings. Contentment is not the pretence that things are right when they are not; instead, it displays the peace that comes from knowing that God is bigger than any problem and that He works them all out for our good. Contentment ensures that our wellbeing, joy, and peace of mind isn't circumstantial, but is focused on God who never varies.

Contentment is not influenced by external circumstances but on an internal source. Contentment is of the heart.

Contentment isn't denying one's feelings about wanting and desiring what they can't have; instead, it exhibits freedom from being controlled by those feelings.

Apostle Paul reminds us that we brought nothing into the world, and we can take nothing out of it (1 Timothy 6:7). According to John Stott (an Anglican Priest and Author), *"Life, in fact, is a pilgrimage from one moment of nakedness to another."* Therefore, we should strive to live a simple life. Simplicity says, *"If we have food and clothing, we will be content with that."* For the genuine Christian, contentment knows that if we have Jesus, we have enough. Sadly, for many Christians today, Jesus isn't enough. He is not the ultimate possession of many; instead, He is just a means to their selfish materialist pursuit.

> Contentment is not influenced by external circumstances but on an internal source. Contentment is of the heart.

Some have confused contentment with complacency; it doesn't mean being satisfied with less. As Christians, we can work to improve our circumstances as we have the opportunity. The Word of God extols hard work and the rewards that come from it (as long as we are free of greed). Being content is finding joy with whatever God has given you per time – not robbing yourself of the enjoyment of what you have or where you are because you are focused on what you do not have. It is an inner sense of peace that comes from being right with God and knowing He is in control of all that happens to you. If God grants us material comforts, we can thankfully enjoy them, knowing it all comes from His loving hand.

But we should also seek to use them for His purposes by being generous. Even when we do not have riches and material comfort, our joy remains intact because we fix our eyes on Him. We do not allow ourselves to be wrongly seduced by prosperity because we centre our lives on a living relationship with the Lord Jesus Christ.

Contentment comes from focusing on God as sovereign, saviour and sufficient. It comes from knowing God as the Sovereign One to whom we must submit, the Saviour whom we must serve and the Sufficient One whom we must trust. If we know Him in these ways (as Paul did), we will know contentment. Unfortunately, we are not born with this state of mind, so it is not natural to us. It is not even a gift. We learn such contentment; learning to trust God explicitly no matter the outcomes. Most people thirst for what Apostle Paul had: enduring-contentment (deep-down, soul-satisfying contentment). That kind of contentment can only come from within. Contentment is always an inside job. It has

> Being content is finding joy with whatever God has given you per time – not robbing yourself of the enjoyment of what you have or where you are because you are focused on what you do not have.

everything to do with what is going on inside you, not what is going on outside. It has only one source, which is found in a soul-satisfying relationship with our Heavenly Father who cares for us and promised to meet us where we are.

Let me ask a question: What is that one thing separating you from joy right now? How do you fill in the blank: "I will be happy when I am ______"? When I am healed? Promoted? Married? Single again? Rich? How would you finish the statement? Now, with your answer firmly in mind, answer this: If your ship never comes in, if your dream never comes true, if the situation never changes, could you be happy? If your response is "No!" then you are living in the claws of discontentment.

I love how Jeremiah Burroughs, a 17th Century Preacher described contentment. He calls it: 'A rare jewel'. Hear his great wisdom on how to get it:

"A Christian comes to contentment, not so much through additions as through subtraction... Contentment does not come by adding to what you have, but by subtracting from what you desire. The world says you will find contentment when your possessions rise to meet the level of your desires... The Christian has another way to contentment, he can bring his desires down to his possessions."

Contentment is a matter of accepting from God's hand what he sends because we know that He is a good God and wants to give good gifts to His children. We accept, therefore, from God's hand that which He provides. All that is

> Discontentment has the potential to destroy our peace, rob us of joy, make us miserable and tarnish our witness.

needful, He will supply. He would even redeem pain and suffering that may seem impossible to correct. If we do not surrender, we will forever be discontent. We will suffocate our own freedom. We will be in bondage to our desires and our relationships will be poisoned with jealousy and competition and we will, eventually, sacrifice our potential happiness and blessings. Discontentment has the potential to destroy our peace, rob us of joy, make us miserable and tarnish our witness. We dishonour God if we proclaim a Saviour who satisfies and yet, live in discontentment. We cannot expect contentment to fall into our laps via education, money, or status. This is because contentment arises from a divine source that money and material possessions cannot purchase.

The secret of contentment is not apparent to a casual observer. But what is that secret?

"For me, living is Christ and dying is gain."[3]

The cornerstone of contentment is the cross – remembering what Jesus has done for us on the cross. Because of the cross, Jesus has set us free from the chains of sin and worldly desires.

We learn contentment, and it takes some time. It's a process that would require us taking one step at a time:

> The cornerstone of contentment is the cross – remembering what Jesus has done for us on the cross.

Step one: Forget the Past.

"Brothers, I do not consider myself to have taken hold. But one thing I do: forgetting what is behind and reaching forward to what is ahead."[4]

We cannot hope to be content while holding unto past failures and mistakes (whether others or ours). There's a difference between ignoring past wrongs and forgetting them. Forgetting means we work through forgiving of others and allow God's forgiveness to cover us. We need to let go of statements that begin with 'I should have…' 'If only…' and 'If they hadn't…'   True forgiveness requires that we see the wrongs, articulate them, release them to God, and then walk away from them. This step may take some time and need some assistance; but without it, we will never have a contented heart.

Step two: Live one Day at a Time.

"And my God will supply all your needs according to His riches in glory in Christ Jesus"[5]

Here, we wait on God. We need to surrender our timetable and future to Him. Discontentment arises because of wrong focus. If we focus on things and on others, we will be discontent. But if we focus on God, living each day in the light of His glory, the things of this earth will pale in comparison.

Step three: Find Sufficiency in Jesus Christ.

"I am able to do all things through Him who strengthens

me."[6]

The term 'content' suggests self-sufficiency. But in this text, it means being at peace with Christ's sufficiency. When His powerful presence consumes us, we can do all things. Christ has given us immense strength, but we can experience contentment because we are continual recipients of His supernatural power. Our human determination may help us endure adversity and pain, our emotional toughness will help us get through job loss and financial hardships, but only Christ can generate a contented spirit within us amidst all that is happening around us.

> Contentment knows that Jesus is enough.

Contentment knows that Jesus is enough. If you know Jesus, you have a God who hears you; you have the power of love behind you; you have the Holy Spirit within you and all of heaven ahead of you. If you have Jesus, you have grace for every sin; direction for every turn; a candle for every corner and an anchor for every storm. You have everything you need!

Chapter Ten

THE COMMONWEALTH

"I am prepared to resort to anything, to
submit to anything, for the sake of
the commonwealth."

Julius Caesar (100 – 44BC)
Former Roman General

The Common-Wealth

Our focus, up to this point, has been on the financial stewardship of the individual and how God expects us as Christians to handle the resources He has committed to our care. Recall also that earlier on (in Chapter 2), I mentioned that most of the arguments about tithing are about the administration and application of the proceeds rather than the concept itself. Therefore, if the individual must learn to relate to money rightly, shouldn't the managers of our common purse do so as well? Doesn't this place greater responsibility on our church leaders? Should church leaders take a second look at how they apply the income from tithes and offerings, or hold the arrogant view that their management is above scrutiny? Would a stitch in time save nine by creating an internal self-regulatory mechanism that ensures that there is a transparent accountability system in place, or should they wait for the government or a 'Pharaoh who doesn't know Joseph', or even congregants to demand and enforce it?

Governments of countries like Rwanda, under Paul Kagame, have already started regulating churches; and not so long ago, the Federal government tested the waters with the Financial Reporting Council (FRC). This idea may seem far-fetched, but if the recent clamour by critics about tithing and the lifestyles of church leaders and the democratization of information because of the growing influence of the Internet (and social media in particular) is anything to go by, those days are not very far away.

If we are to be honest, the Church in Nigeria has lost a measure of respect and awe. Perhaps, many may even consider that an understatement. Our leaders are no longer as revered as they used to be, both within and outside the church community. If you listen long enough, the feedback you will get (especially from the much younger generation) is that the Church is no longer adding value. For many today, the Church is a 'taker' or a 'user'. All she makes are demands and more demands – adding no real value. The Church is doing a lot; **especially the Catholic church**, but perhaps, too little compared to what the whole body can do and what people expect.

The prosperity message and the way many preached it for a long time created this mindset or influenced the expectations of many. The economic conditions were very harsh in the early 80's and the introduction of the "Structural Adjustment Program (SAP)" pulverized most Nigerians; it decimated businesses, and it was all a tale of doom and gloom. People were at their wits' end. It was in the middle of this turmoil that the Lord gave the Church the prosperity message. I personally believe it was a message from God. Whether it was adequately taught or abused is a different subject altogether. For many, this message of hope and prosperity was a burst of sunshine in an era of hopelessness as millions of people, especially in the South, trooped into churches. Holding spaces became too small to accommodate the new converts; therefore, abandoned warehouses of decimated factories (owing to the harsh economic conditions) were bought over by the rapidly expanding churches to create room for new converts.

The revival was well and underway in Nigeria. As revival swept through the country in the mid-eighties and early nineties, the Church grew, especially the Pentecostal/Evangelical denominations. The outpouring led to the most significant church growth ever experienced in the country, and as a result, the Nigerian Church gained international attention. As the elites joined the Church, they demanded and got marketplace quality in infrastructure, delivery, and ambience.

Then, things took a turn. The focus on making it bigger, smoother, and slicker became the preoccupation of the modern-day Church. Churches foist on themselves expansion projects and financial targets that were unreasonable and sometimes, unrealistic. Besides, the lifestyle of church leaders also changed to match the new look, while crafting sermons to justify their rock star status. Unfortunately, the mixed messages eventually confused the congregation about what it means to be spiritual. Materialism took firm roots in the Church, and material possessions became a barometer for measuring spirituality and God's favour. The flashy cars, the impressive mansions and the expensive clothes became signs of God's blessings. In a society dominated by the greedy and populated by the deprived, the ignorant and the destitute, it is easy to see how the materialistic gospel can quickly become the gospel of the majority. This is so because we live in a flamboyant society – a society that worships wealth, money or possession. The increasing worldliness of our society today is such that a focused preacher (one of a rare breed, today) who devotes more than a few sentences talking about heaven and hell and good

> In a society dominated by the greedy and populated by the deprived, the ignorant and the destitute, it is easy to see how the materialistic gospel can quickly become the gospel of the majority.

character, and less about God's readiness to give us unlimited prosperity, is probably unlikely to keep a viable congregation for any reasonable length of time.

Many church leaders may randomly dismiss these points of view, but this is the perception even among some faithful. There is a sense among the silent minority that materialism, opportunism, and vainglory have taken front seats; and the pre-occupation with prosperity and instant gratifications have left no air for the Nigerian Church to breathe. The prosperity message is skewed. There was, and might still be, no emphasis on prudence, contentment, accountability, social good and a clear definition of the purpose of material blessings from God. Therefore, in my humble opinion, this message did more harm than good. It not only fanned the ambers of greed and discontentment in clear violation of the true essence of the gospel but reduced Christianity to a mere financial transaction.

Some false doctrines that came out of the prosperity message include:

1. Congregants were taught that the local assembly was synonymous with the Kingdom. Therefore, the kingdom of God starts and ends with their local assembly. Church leaders continue to teach the gospel of salvation rather than the gospel of the kingdom. Therefore, soul-winning is confused with the expansion of the kingdom.

2. The promotion of sowing (giving to your local assembly & Pastor) and reaping as the primary means to financial increase have reduced *following Jesus* to a mere commercial transaction. People were also made to believe that they couldn't prosper beyond the degree to which their pastor and the ministry thrived. In other words, their progress in life was irreversibly tied to the progress or increase that the leader and ministry enjoy at any time. If they refuse to give to the church, they inadvertently limit or deny themselves of prosperity.

3. Wealth was (and is still) considered proof of God's blessing regardless of how it was obtained. The obscene display of wealth by both church leaders and members has helped stoke the flames of greed and materialism.

4. The instant gratification promised by the sowing-and-reaping or the 'name it, claim it, and grab it'-mentality relegated genuine hard work to the background.

5. Stewardship and accountability were reduced to tithing and giving to church projects no matter how vain and unrealistic they are.

These things are still being taught in many places, overtly or covertly, and prominent leaders ought to do more to correct these false teachings. The Church is the salt of the earth – so the Bible says. Salt was used as a preservative in those days. The purpose of the Church is to save the world from decay; not mimic it. But in order to save the world, we must be in contact with the world; yet, differ from the world. You need not become a monkey to catch a monkey.

Why should the Church struggle to make a difference in a land of widespread rot where a difference could be made by doing little? I think the Body of Christ in Nigeria is not as effective as it should be because we may have gotten our priorities wrong.

I believe the church should return to its social roots by applying the bulk of her income to social services that alleviate suffering and poverty while discipling the nations.

Chapter Eleven

THE GREAT COMMISSION

"Go out and train everyone you meet,
far and near, in this way of life..."

Jesus Christ

The Great Commission

I have heard people, including church leaders, say the bane of the Church (the body of Christ in Nigeria) is that it doesn't have means or enough money to be as influential as it should be. I disagree. The Church has a considerate amount of money to be very influential and effective in prosecuting the Great Commission. Unverified figures making the rounds in different circles estimate that the Nigerian Church generates over two trillion Naira annually.

For those who are not familiar with the mandate of the Church, it is in Matthew 28:19-20. These two verses contain what we commonly call 'The Great Commission' – Our Lord's marching orders to His disciples after His resurrection. The most common interpretation of this verse, perhaps, requires a second look.

The way it is interpreted (at least in practice) is this: *"Do whatever is possible to get an unbeliever to say the 'Sinner's Prayer' and then enrol them in a church for discipleship. If you do a good job, then you will get more and more people into a building for fellowship twice or thrice a week."* This is what this thinking would look like in a Bible verse: *"For God so loved Christians that He gave His only begotten Son, therefore go into the world and make disciples of all Christians..."*

The current practice prioritizes making disciples of 'Christians' rather than making disciples of the 'nations' as Jesus commanded. I believe that what Jesus instructed His disciples to do is to go and teach the world how to live; to make the principles and values of the kingdom the mainstream of culture, rather than the subset it is today.

Myles Munroe, author of Kingdom Principles, describes a kingdom in these terms:

"A kingdom is the governing influence of a king over his territory, impacting it with his personal will, purpose, and intent, producing a culture, values, morals and lifestyle that reflects the king's desire and nature for his citizens."

Jesus' desire is for God's kingdom to be manifested on earth. When He taught the disciples to pray, He taught them to petition their heavenly Father by asking,

"Your kingdom come. Your will be done on earth as it is in heaven."[1]

If we continue to make this mistake of exclusively discipling individuals, we would miss the higher prize of discipling nations. We would have to choose between being changed by the world or being world changers.

What do you think is the purpose of television programs like: Keeping up with the Kardashians, Big Brother, etc.? These programs are not just for entertainment anymore, reality TV is the new way the world teaches (disciples) people – including church folks (who are in church week-in, week-out) on how to live. The children of this world are wiser than ever; they veil messages (that would otherwise be considered offensive) with entertainment and make them subliminal. They occupy our conscious mind with the fun of entertainment while targeting our subconscious mind with the fiery darts of the world system. Entertainment is used to distract, lower our defences and deaden our sensibilities, while doing the damage.

The shallow interpretation of the Great Commission is what I believe has robbed the church of the clarity it requires for executing the grand vision of Christ and may even be

> Entertainment is used to distract, lower our defences and deaden our sensibilities, while doing the damage.

responsible for the current timid approach to evangelism. Jesus created the Church to be a world-changer; but sadly, there is no way to achieve this through the current model of 'churching'.

We need a new paradigm on how we steward our resources today. The truth, I insist, is that the Church has extensive resources and high potentials for unlocking an even greater reservoir. What is lacking, in my opinion, is a strategic vision undergirded by a rightly interpreted 'Great Commission.'

If the job of Jesus' disciples is to disciple the world, then it means we must look beyond church buildings and not be so fixated on weekly meetings. We must seek influence across all veins of culture. We must leave the comfort and confinement of the four walls of buildings and target the critical channels of culture.

Pop culture has captured the imagination of people everywhere; dictating and dominating the way of life of many around the world through music, drama, film, games, fashion, new and old mass media. Countries of the world seeking to limit the influence of other cultures have always targeted these channels. The world system has successfully pushed its agendas (like the gay movement, abortion, and so on) by using subliminal messages in programs throughout the mass media, which the Church has ceded almost wholly and exclusively.

The Church can no longer wait for people to come to her. Like Jesus, the Church must go where people spend most of their 168-hour week. Let's do a little math: for how long can you hold people in a building in weekly meetings? Maybe four or five hours a week. So, where do they spend the remaining 163 hours? Who are they watching or listening to? Whoever or whatever it is they are watching, listening to, and spending those remaining hours with, ultimately shapes their thoughts and controls their lives.

The constant bashing of culture is a lazy and complacent approach to getting the job done. Rather than a complaint about the entrenched influence of culture, the Church must step up and compete for the hearts and souls of men in places where values, beliefs, and lifestyles are shaped. The prophet Isaiah says,

"The Spirit of the Lord is upon Me, Because the Lord has anointed me to preach the good tidings to the poor; He has sent Me to heal the broken-hearted, To proclaim liberty to captives, And the opening of prison to those who are bound; to proclaim the acceptable year of the Lord, And the day of vengeance of our God; To comfort all who mourn."[2]

These three verses are very popular among church leaders. Many have traced their call to ministry to these verses. Therefore, several churches and ministries have been founded on them. Those words became even more popular when our Lord Jesus quoted them (in Luke 4) as His ministry mandate.

I have a couple of questions:

- What happens when revival hits and we are anointed? When the captives have been set free and the ugliness of ashes replaced with beauty?
- What happens after the Saints have been redeemed and equipped for the work of ministry? What is even the work of ministry?

I believe that the main work of ministry can be found in the next verse:

"And they shall rebuild the old ruins, they shall raise up the former desolations, and they shall repair the ruined cities, the desolation of many generations."[4]

Personal redemption is the beginning of our participation in God's work of restoration in our lives and in the world and that's what verses 1-3 was about but Jesus came to the earth to restore all that was lost in the Garden of Eden and gave the keys back to man for him to reclaim and transform.

The church must unleash a new breed of Missionaries, Sovereign-sent 'Carpenters' who are not limited by geographic boundaries or the narrow definitions of ministry; men and women who will take the gospel into all channels of culture and spheres where the devil is currently unchallenged in order for Christ to build His

Church.

For us to realize the grand vision of our Lord Jesus Christ, we need to start developing and executing culture-shifting ideas. We need to promote an alternative culture that offers people an option to the prevailing world ideologies and systems. Therefore, there is the need to redesign the evangelism model and redirect budgets away from elaborate buildings and traditional television and radio programming; to, competing for airtime on prime-time TV, box office, and new media content with deliberate, well-crafted subliminal messages in an out-of-the-box approach.

With the rapid growth of the Internet, how many people will gather for a traditional church service 20 years from now? Today, more and more people prefer to join church service online; so, what will happen to our cathedrals?

One of the most common refrains you hear in Christian circles these days is the fact that people of other faith have an agenda. And the question I keep asking is this: Who stopped us from having one of our own? Rather than complain and gripe about the agenda of others and what they are doing, why don't we develop a grand agenda of our own? What is wrong with developing a strategic plan to grow the body of Christ in Nigeria by ten million people over the next ten years through the different veins of culture? We need visionaries who would look at the entire playing field, beyond our well-touted crumbs (like the number of people we gather weekly and the coolness of our facilities and the sleekness of our services, and the platforms we are invited to speak), to craft a bold vision for the entire body or even our local assemblies.

Take education for instance, the government ruined the system by taking over missionary schools in 1977. Before then, 60 to 70% of primary and secondary schools were owned by Christian organizations or churches and there was little or no 'sorting' and exam malpractices, cultism or incessant strikes. When the light was taken out of our schools, darkness took over. Why can't we envision growing the Church in Nigeria by five million people of the ten-million-target in ten years through the vein of education alone? Not by building denominational schools to generate extra income, or starting elitist schools that church members can't even afford; but by viewing our poorly funded and dilapidated public schools as our new mission fields.

Imagine what might happen if a local assembly, or two, come together (moved by the sheer love of Christ) to adopt a rundown public school and upgrade and transform it into a modern learning centre. We can then seize the opportunity to create a permanent platform for sharing the gospel of Jesus in non-threatening ways. These kinds of projects will not only change the current narrative and perception of the Church but also ensure that there is a deliberate plan in place to keep the Church growing well into the future. The fact that the Church has a great message is not enough; it must earn the right to be heard. This was how the first-century Church spread the gospel with no printed sacred documents or buildings. Say what you like, but this was how Nigeria was evangelized by Europe – They built schools; vocational training centres, shelters, hospital etc. and everyone had access for free. It's time for us to return to our social roots in a big way.

Reason with me for a moment, how did the gay movement (a word and practice that could only be spoken about behind firmly shut doors a few years ago) become annual festivals in almost every major city of the world? Why is sexual immorality such a commonplace affair today; so much that we now live in a sexually charged society? Well, just in case you live on another planet, the answer is through music, movies, television, and fashion. They have perfected how to use these mediums to promote whatever they want society to adopt as acceptable practices. These are today's discipleship platforms of the world. This was the purpose of the Church founded by Jesus Christ; but unfortunately, we are now content with just huddling in meetings to disciple fellow Christians rather than the world.

> The fact that the Church has a great message is not enough; it must earn the right to be heard.

Can you imagine what would happen if the Church decides to start producing high-quality sitcoms and soaps (that promote ethical family values) for prime-time viewing, rather than what is currently being aired (which encourages infidelity, divorce, violence, etc.)? Imagine what would happen if the Church galvanizes her base to start the production of films of exportable quality with a distinct Christian worldview.

I had the pleasure of watching the *Passion of the Christ* in Odeon Cinema in central London shortly after it was released in April 2004, and I was struck by the number of people who left the cinema in tears – many of whom have never read the Bible or been in a church building in all their lives. This low budget film became the 7th highest grossing film. It reminded me right there that, truly, people are hopelessly lost without the gospel, but only few will show up at our churches. Imagine that we had several movies of that quality on a back-to-back basis in cinema houses, what do you think will happen? It is fifteen years since the Passion of the Christ, and nothing of that standard has been put out again.

I think we need a new breed of Apostles and Evangelists who are so, not by a title, but by what they do in a brave new world; people who would take the gospel to places (veins of cultural) where Christ is not named.

What might happen when the Church develops this kind of bold, high-impact culture-shifting vision for her congregations? I can guess what would happen:

- It would attract and engage a good number of millennials who are turning their back on the Church in droves. These are the ones who question the relevance of the Church today and have become slaves to entertainment and new media.

- A bold, recalibrated evangelism vision will tap into the knowledge-base of the current and future generations. It would attract, engage and unleash the talents and skills of this largest un-churched demography while transforming lives.

- It will draw, not just more people, but new source of donations and funding from even those outside the Church.

These and more will make the Church more influential and respected in the community. The Church must see the entire world as its playing field– rather than a few square meters' spaces within any walls.

Conclusion

Conclusion

This book has spoken to different subjects and audiences within the body of Christ and maybe even beyond but I want to conclude by being clear on what I believe that we should do individually as church leaders, members and congregants and collectively as the church of Christ.

THE CONGREGANTS

"Then we shall no longer be children, carried by the waves and blown about by every shifting wind of teaching of deceitful people who lead others into error by the tricks they invent"[1]

Many Christians today fall into the second category of those that Jesus talked about in the parable of the sower in Mathew 13. The condition of their heart is like that of a stony place. They have no depth therefore they are shallow and fickle; they are tossed around by every wind of doctrine.

Since the tithe argument broke many simply found a perfect excuse to withhold their generosity to their churches but sadly it wasn't out of any conviction or knowledge from personal study. While I recognize that many church leaders are fleecing their congregation and exploiting their members, the people cannot exonerate themselves of the sin of the worship of their men of God and the lack of scholarliness and devotion to study of their Bible and knowing God for themselves. Therefore they became gullible and easily swayed by all sorts of doctrines.

As you have learned in this book tithing is not compulsory but generosity is, and the giving standards in the New Testament are even higher than the requirements of the Old Testament. Giving is important for the many reasons I have mentioned across the entire book. Therefore you should plan your giving and support genuine work of God and the vulnerable around you.

God is not a means to your financial goal and He is not one of the condiments you throw into your life's "pot of soup" so as to make it more delicious. God is the end to which all things must serve as a tool of devotion:

including your money.

Let me remind you of a powerful promise of the Bible. It says if you handle worldly wealth well (according to His plan), God will entrust you with "true riches"

TO THE UN-CHURCHED

If you are a believer but not committed to a local assembly you are not in full alignment with God's word. So find a good church and be planted there. God wants you to belong to a spiritual family where you can be cared for and care for others and your soul can be nourished.

If you are a footballer you must belong to a team. You cannot say you just play in the Nigerian premier league and not belong to a team in the league. The church is a body and we function as teams.

"For just as the body is one and has many members, and all the members of the body, though many are one body, so it is with Christ...If one member suffers, all suffer together; if one member is honoured, all rejoice together. Now you are the body of Christ and individually members of it"[2]

Here is my advice, when seeking a place of worship do your due diligence. Seek God's guidance. Know what the church believes; look out for integrity and transparency in the leadership. I am not asking you to seek for perfection, nobody is and you are not either. Once you are convinced that you are in the right place, plug in and be a blessing.

TO OUR CHURCH LEADERS

Church leaders must abandon the narrow fixation on obligatory giving (tithing) and point their congregations to the extravagant giving of the cross. We must teach people to be generous and be contented and in doing so lead by example. We must refocus members on Christ and the riches in Him rather than doctrines that promote worldly riches, greed and the relentless glorification of a life of luxury. The doctrine that says that the blessing of Abraham is mainly earthly riches isn't true; the blessing of Abraham is justification by faith in Christ Jesus. Any gospel contrary to this only feeds the flesh and not the Spirit. As I have said before, being a Christian means being changed from inside out so that you fall in love with God and people and fall out of love with things.

It is true that God wants us to be rich but just not in the way you think and not in the way many have taught it. The Bible tells us in unmistakeable terms that Jesus is rich and He came to share His riches with us but His riches are not in mere silver or gold or paper currencies. The value of worldly wealth pales in comparison to the true riches of Christ. This is where the prosperity message falls short because it emphasises worldly wealth instead of the true riches of Christ and because of that the rightful place of Christ in the heart of many Christians has been displaced by mammon.

The true riches of Christ which include genuine freedom from the power of sin and death, right standing with God and others, joy, peace, etc. here on earth and an eternal life of bliss at the end of the age with the risen Christ; all these outweigh the glory of worldly wealth.

Church leaders must learn to cast a compelling vision for their churches about what God wants to do in them, with them and through them. If the vision is of the Spirit and it is clear, it will attract provision. If it's of God there would be no need to manipulate people to give, God himself with provide for His vision because *"on the mountain of the Lord it shall be seen"* (Jehovah Jireh).

Pastors must learn to develop Big Hairy Audacious Goal (BHAG) that emphasises building and transforming people and impacting popular culture with the gospel rather than construction projects.

They should tamper their penchant for extravagant and flamboyant lifestyle and ensue modesty as the Bible teaches.

Remember that you will give account for every member and every word you preached before the Judgement seat of Christ.

Note: Shortly before going to the press to print this

book I was invited to the launch of a new association by a group of church leaders and professionals who have also become concerned about the issue of accountability and proper corporate governance in the body. The new association is a self-regulatory body of churches and Christian organisation called Christian Financial Accountability Association (CFAA).

I foresee a time soon when many Christians will no longer support any ministry without proper governance and accountability no matter how 'anointed' its leader might be.

TO THE UNBELIEVER

Jesus Christ loves you. He loves you so much that He came into the world to die for you. His death on the cross is a substitutionary payment for all the sins and the wrongs you have ever done or will ever commit. Therefore, if you accept His sacrifice by faith, all your sins are wiped away and you are declared righteous. In this world you are guaranteed of peace with God and a promise of a life of bliss with Him in eternity.

Christianity is not a religion; it's a relationship. In order to help you develop a close relationship with Him, Jesus will come and dwell in you through His Spirit who will teach you how to live henceforth.

And if you will like to say yes to Him right now, I would

like to pray with you. Please say this simple prayer:

"Dear Lord Jesus, I acknowledge that I am a sinner, and I ask for Your forgiveness. I believe You died for my sins and rose from the dead. I turn from my sins and turn my heart and life over to You. I want to trust and follow You as my Lord and Saviour. Thank You for saving me. Amen!"

If you just said that prayer and need further information about your next step, please call us on: +2348189360970 or send an email to: info@TonyAleogena.org

REFERENCES

Chapter 1

1.   Ecclesiastes 10:19 (New King James Version)
2.   Luke 16:1 (New King James Version)
3.   Luke 16:1-13 (New King James Version)
4.   Deuteronomy 8:11-18 (New King James Version)
5.   1 Chronicles 29:12-14 (New King James Version)
6.   Luke 16:2 (New King James Version)
7.   1 Corinthians 4:2 (New King James Version)
8.   Matthew 25:14-30 (God's Word Translation)
9.   Luke 16:8 - 9 (New King James Version)
10.   Matthew 5:19 (New King James Version)
11.   1 Timothy 6:17 (New King James Version)
12.   Luke 16:10 - 12 (New King James Version)
13.   Matthew 25:29 (New Living Translation)
14.   Luke 16:15 (New King James Version)

Chapter 2

1.   Malachi 3:8-10 (New King James Version)
2.   Ephesians 4:28 (New International Version)
3.   Leviticus 19:9-10 (New International Version)
4.   Leviticus 27:30-32 (New King James Version)
5.   Numbers 18:21 (New International Version)
6.   Romans 8:16-17 (New King James Version)
7.   Deuteronomy 14:22-23 (New International

Version)

8.   Deuteronomy 14:28-29 (New King James Version)

9.   Acts 4:32-35 (New King James Version)

10.   Hebrews 12:15 (New International Version)

11.   Matthew 23:23 and Luke 11:42 (New King James Version)

12.   Mark 12:41-44 (New King James Version)

13.   2 Corinthians 8:8 (New King James Version)

14.   James 2:15-16 (New King James Version)

15.   1 Corinthians 9:13-14 (New King James Version)

16.   1 Timothy 5:17-18 (New King James Version)

17.   Galatians 6:6 (New King James Version)

18.   Adam Clarke Commentaries on 1 Corinthians 9

Chapter 3

1.   Luke 12:16-21 (New King James Version)

2.   John 12:3-6 (New King James Version)

3.   Matthew 6:22-23 (New King James Version)

4.   Matthew 6:19-21 (New King James Version)

5.   Proverbs 13:12 (New King James Version)

6.   Ecclesiastes 5:10 (New International Version)

7.   Proverbs 22:7 (New International Version)

8.   Psalms 37:21 (New King James Version)

Chapter 4

1.   1 Timothy 5:8 (New King James Version)

2.   Romans 12:2 (Message Bible)

3.   Ecclesiastics 5:11 (New King James Version)
4.   Proverbs 21:5 (New Living Translation)
5.   1 Timothy 6:8 (New King James Version)
6.   Proverbs 6:6-8 (Good News Bible)
7.   Proverb 13:11 (New International Version)
8.   Proverbs 13:22 (New International Version)
9.   1 Timothy 6:17 (New International Version)
10.   Habakkuk 2:2-3 (Message Bible)
11.   Proverbs 22:7 (New King James Version)
12.   Proverbs 15:22 (New King James Version)
13.   2 Corinthians 9:8 (New King James Version)

Chapter 5

1.   Acts 4:36-37 (New King James Version)
2.   Acts 5:1-3 (New King James Version)
3.   Luke 19:5 (English Standard Version)
4.   Luke 19:8 (English Standard Version)
5.   Luke 19:9 (English Standard Version)
6.   2 Corinthians 8:1 (English Standard Version)
7.   2 Corinthians 8:4 (New International Version)
8.   2 Corinthians 8:1-5 (New King James Version)
9.   2 Corinthians 8:9 (New King James Version)
10.   Matthew 6:25-34 (New International Version)
11.   Matthew 16:19 (New King James Version)

Chapter 6

1.   1 Timothy 6:17 (New King James Version)
2.   Proverb 18:11 (New International Version)

3.   Mark 10:17-22 (New King James Version)
4.   Proverbs 23:5 (Easy to Read Version)
5.   Ecclesiastes 5:10 (New International Version)
6.   Luke 21:3-4 (New King James Version)
7.   Mark 12:41-44 (New International Version)
8.   Exodus 36:2-7 (New King James Version)
9.   2 Corinthians 8:1-5
10.   Matthew 25:35-37 (New King James Version)
11.   Proverbs 11:24 (New International Version)
12.   Matthew 6:19 (New King James Version)

Chapter 8

1.   Acts 20:35 (New International Version)
2.   2 Corinthians 9:7 (New King James Version)
3.   Acts 2:45-47 (New International Version)
4.   In 2 Corinthians 9:10 (New International Version)

Chapter 9

1.   Philippians 4:12 (New International Version)
2.   1 Timothy 6:6 (New King James Version)
3.   Philippians 1:21 (Holman Christian Standard Bible)
4.   Philippians 3:13 (Holman Christian Standard Bible)
5.   Philippians 4:19 (Holman Christian Standard Bible)
6.   Philippians 4:13 (Holman Christian Standard

Bible)

Chapter 11

1.   Matthew 6:10 (New King James Version)
2.   Isaiah 61:1-3 (New King James Version)
3.   Isaiah 61:4 (New King James Version)

Conclusion

1.   Ephesians 4:14 (Good News Bible)
2.   1 Corinthians 12:12-27 (English Standard Version)